EMOTIONS

JOURNEY THROUGH THE MIND AND BODY

TIME®
LIFE
BOOKS

Other Publications:
WEIGHT WATCHERS® SMART CHOICE RECIPE COLLECTION
TRUE CRIME
THE AMERICAN INDIANS
THE ART OF WOODWORKING
LOST CIVILIZATIONS
ECHOES OF GLORY
THE NEW FACE OF WAR
HOW THINGS WORK
WINGS OF WAR
CREATIVE EVERYDAY COOKING
COLLECTOR'S LIBRARY OF THE UNKNOWN
CLASSICS OF WORLD WAR II
TIME-LIFE LIBRARY OF CURIOUS AND UNUSUAL FACTS
AMERICAN COUNTRY
VOYAGE THROUGH THE UNIVERSE
THE THIRD REICH
THE TIME-LIFE GARDENER'S GUIDE
MYSTERIES OF THE UNKNOWN
TIME FRAME
FIX IT YOURSELF
FITNESS, HEALTH & NUTRITION
SUCCESSFUL PARENTING
HEALTHY HOME COOKING
UNDERSTANDING COMPUTERS
LIBRARY OF NATIONS
THE ENCHANTED WORLD
THE KODAK LIBRARY OF CREATIVE PHOTOGRAPHY
GREAT MEALS IN MINUTES
THE CIVIL WAR
PLANET EARTH
COLLECTOR'S LIBRARY OF THE CIVIL WAR
THE EPIC OF FLIGHT
THE GOOD COOK
WORLD WAR II
HOME REPAIR AND IMPROVEMENT
THE OLD WEST

*For information on and a full description of any of
the Time-Life Books series listed above, please call*
1-800-621-7026 *or write*:
Reader Information
Time-Life Customer Service
P.O. Box C-32068
Richmond, Virginia 23261-2068

EMOTIONS

JOURNEY THROUGH THE MIND AND BODY

BY THE EDITORS OF TIME-LIFE BOOKS
ALEXANDRIA, VIRGINIA

CONSULTANTS:

MARGARET CLARK has edited many publications on emotions and social psychology; her own research focuses on mood, emotions, and behavior. She teaches at Carnegie-Mellon University in Pittsburgh.

DOUGLAS DERRYBERRY's special research interests in psychology are emotions and motivation. He teaches at Oregon State University.

PAUL EKMAN teaches psychology at the University of California in San Francisco and studies human emotions and non-verbal communication at the university's Human Interaction Laboratory.

LAWRENCE A. FARWELL, a neuroscientist, is director and chief scientist at the Human Brain Research Laboratory, Inc., in Bethesda, Maryland.

CARROLL IZARD teaches psychology at the University of Delaware. He has studied and analyzed the facial expressions of infants.

ROBERT PLUTCHIK teaches psychology at the Albert Einstein College of Medicine; he developed a structural model of emotions.

CAROL TAVRIS is a social psychologist. She writes and lectures from Los Angeles, where she lives.

JOURNEY THROUGH THE MIND AND BODY

Time-Life Books is a division of
Time Life Inc.

PRESIDENT AND CEO: John M. Fahey Jr.
EDITOR-IN-CHIEF: John L. Papanek

TIME-LIFE BOOKS

MANAGING EDITOR: Roberta Conlan

Executive Art Director: Ellen Robling
Director of Photography and Research:
John Conrad Weiser
Senior Editors: Russell B. Adams Jr., Dale
M. Brown, Janet Cave, Lee Hassig,
Robert Somerville, Henry Woodhead
Director of Technology: Eileen Bradley
Director of Editorial Operations: Prudence G.
Harris
Library: Louise D. Forstall

PRESIDENT: John D. Hall

Vice President, Director of Marketing:
Nancy K. Jones
Vice President, New Product Development:
Neil Kagan
Vice President, Book Production: Marjann
Caldwell
Production Manager: Marlene Zack

SERIES EDITOR: Robert Somerville
Administrative Editor: Judith W. Shanks

Editorial Staff for *Emotions*
Art Directors: Robert K. Herndon, Dale
Pollekoff, Barbara M. Sheppard, Fatima
Taylor
Picture Editor: Tina S. McDowell
Text Editors: Carl A. Posey (principal), Darcie
Conner Johnston
Associate Editors/Research and Writing: Mark
Galan, Curtis Kopf, Jennifer Mendelsohn,
Narisara Murray
Senior Copyeditor: Donna D. Carey
Editorial Assistant: Kris Dittman
Picture Coordinator: Paige Henke

Special Contributors:
George Constable, Juli Duncan, Laura
Foreman, Patrick Huyghe, Barbara Mallen,
Gina Maranto, Eliot Marshall (text); Elaine
Friebele, Ann Perry, Eugenia S. Scharf,
Susan Gregory Thomas (research); Barbara
L. Klein (index); John Drummond (design).

Correspondents:
Elisabeth Kraemer-Singh (Bonn); Robert
Kroon (Geneva); Marlin Levin (Jerusalem);
Christine Hinze (London); Christina
Lieberman (New York); Maria Vincenza
Aloisi (Paris); Ann Natanson (Rome); Mary
Johnson (Stockholm); Dick Berry (Tokyo).
Valuable assistance was also provided by
Daniel Donnelly (New York).

**Library of Congress
Cataloging-in-Publication Data**
Emotions: journey through the mind and
body / by the editors of Time-Life
Books.
p. cm.— (Journey through the mind and
body)
Includes bibliographical references and
index.
ISBN 0-7835-1060-8
1. Emotions 2. Affect (Psychology).
I. Time-Life Books. II. Series.
BF511.E57 1994
152.4— dc20   94-8885

First printing. Printed in U.S.A.
Published simultaneously in Canada.
School and library distribution by
Time-Life Education, P.O. Box 85026,
Richmond, Virginia 23285-5026.

TIME-LIFE is a trademark of Time Warner
Inc. U.S.A.

This volume is one of a series that
explores the fascinating inner universe
of the human mind and body.

CONTENTS

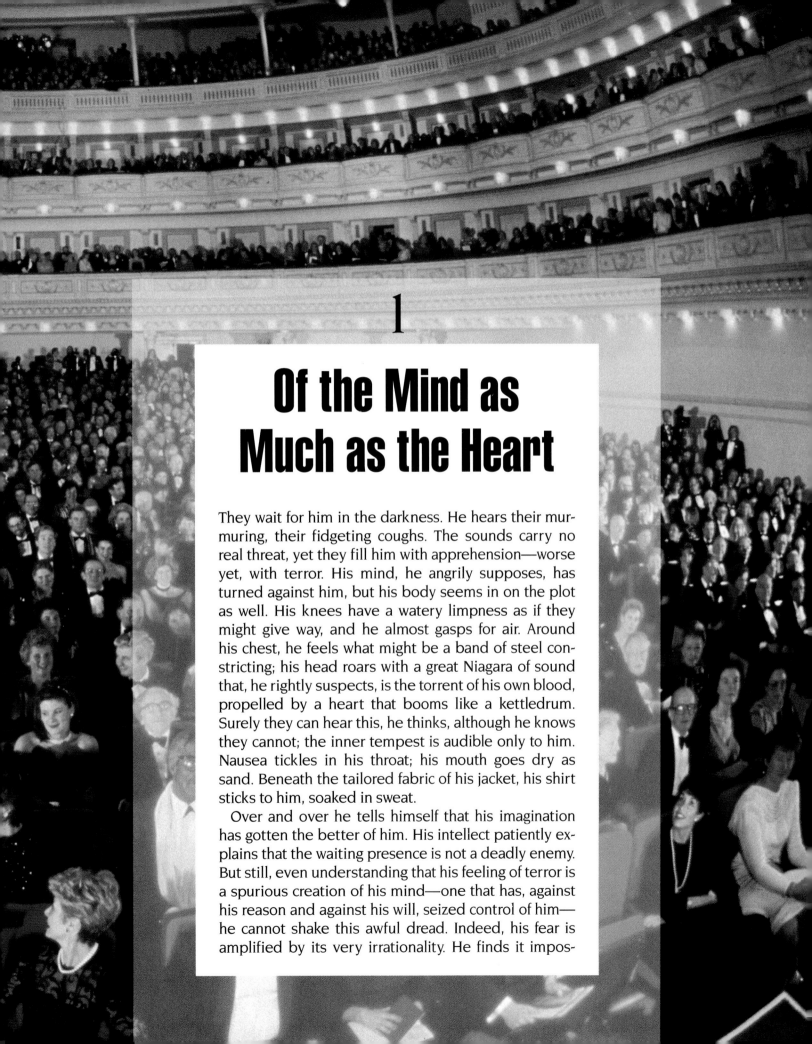

1

Of the Mind as Much as the Heart

They wait for him in the darkness. He hears their murmuring, their fidgeting coughs. The sounds carry no real threat, yet they fill him with apprehension—worse yet, with terror. His mind, he angrily supposes, has turned against him, but his body seems in on the plot as well. His knees have a watery limpness as if they might give way, and he almost gasps for air. Around his chest, he feels what might be a band of steel constricting; his head roars with a great Niagara of sound that, he rightly suspects, is the torrent of his own blood, propelled by a heart that booms like a kettledrum. Surely they can hear this, he thinks, although he knows they cannot; the inner tempest is audible only to him. Nausea tickles in his throat; his mouth goes dry as sand. Beneath the tailored fabric of his jacket, his shirt sticks to him, soaked in sweat.

Over and over he tells himself that his imagination has gotten the better of him. His intellect patiently explains that the waiting presence is not a deadly enemy. But still, even understanding that his feeling of terror is a spurious creation of his mind—one that has, against his reason and against his will, seized control of him— he cannot shake this awful dread. Indeed, his fear is amplified by its very irrationality. He finds it impos-

sible to believe that he could be more frightened than this.

Nevertheless, he steels himself to what he must do. Like a soldier at the front, he follows duty into harm's way. He runs a clammy hand over his hair and tries to wet his lips with his arid tongue, surprised that he can stand, much less walk. He clears his throat, hoping that a voice still lives there, and as if he were about to leap from a high window, plunges through the curtains onto the stage. "Good evening, ladies and gentlemen," he says to the sea of expectant faces beyond the footlights. Even as he speaks, the tide of fear magically recedes.

Stage fright, which is the popular term for such near-paralyzing nervousness, offers a perfect model for what

emotions—*affect*, as Austrian psychoanalyst Sigmund Freud called them—can do to the human mind and body. According to some researchers, about 85 percent of Americans suffer the racing pulse, stomach butterflies, trembling hands, and parched mouth of stage fright whenever they are called upon to appear before a group in public. The response mimics what happens in the face of such tangible threats as the charge of a rabid Doberman or the slipperiness of a mountain road in a blizzard.

Some people claim that stage fright is more fearsome to them than death

itself. Such declarations—overstated though they may be—offer strong testimony to the power of emotion in our lives. More often than we might like to admit, perhaps, it is emotion, and not logic, that rules us.

In simple terms, emotions are the feelings of the mind, the equivalent of what physical sensations are to the body. They are the choreography and currency of human interaction, the resonating mental echo of the external world. Although informed by experience and intellect, they can be irrational, a kind of turbulence in the smoother currents of thought. Emotions seem to be something the mind does to itself—and some would even say inflicts upon itself.

Emotions are exactly what we think

VISIBLY MOVED. This powerfully evocative photograph—taken in Uganda in 1980 and showing the healthy hand of an Italian priest gently cradling the tiny, withered hand of a starving African boy—captures both the pitiless cruelty of famine and the essence of human compassion. Such images can give rise to as strong an emotional response in viewers as an event or scene witnessed in person.

they are: the flush of adolescent desire, the throat-constricting awe evoked by the Grand Canyon, the painful longing for a loved one, the empty ache of loss. Emotions are terrors and elations, griefs and rages, adorations and revulsions, the spasms of mental sensation that cause the heart to leap or wither, that balance hope against despair, that illuminate or cloud the human countenance.

Although emotions are rooted deep in our evolutionary history, thinkers down through the ages have treated them as an anomaly to be shunned or suppressed. In Greek myth, many of the ills that plagued humankind were creatures of emotion—envy, spite, revenge—released into the world by the first woman, Pandora. When the biblical Eve tasted the fruit of Eden's tree of knowledge, she exiled the human race to the turbulently emotional realm beyond the garden. The Ten Commandments given to Moses on the mountain include bans on envy, lust, lying, cursing, stealing, and murder—all linked to the darker, emotional side of human nature.

The world's most revered contemplatives, Gautama Buddha among them, have seen that dark side as the source of all conscious pain. According to the teachings of the Buddha, to be at peace is to be freed from one's restless sensibility. Indeed, for those who have lost control of their feelings —schizophrenics snared by paranoid fears, depressives locked into grinding self-hatred, manics soaring on false joy—emotion may seem a cruel slave master. But in those who have little or no affect, the absence of emotion leaves a terrible empty place.

In fact, few of us would willingly abandon the feelings that so animate the body and fire the mind. For the vast majority of humans, living *is* feeling; to be without emotion is to be cold at the center, to be dead. No matter how they may lead us astray or complicate our existence, emotions have an immediacy and a pungency that tidier rational thought does not.

Literature offers abundant evidence of this. Propelled by raw ambition, then racked by dread and guilt, Shakespeare's Lady Macbeth scrubs neurotically at hands she cannot quite cleanse of blood. Gustave Flaubert's Emma Bovary, tossed by the storms of erotic passion, is swept to a terrible end by her unrelenting desires. Fyodor Dostoyevsky's Karamazov brothers fairly glow with different emotions, one radiant with innocent joy, another plunged in a perpetual brooding anger. Great fictional characters linger in the minds of readers almost in di-

rect proportion to the degree that they embody and evoke certain feelings. So too it is in the real world: People and events are indelibly seared in memory whenever emotions enter the picture.

As pervasive and important as they may be in everyday affairs, emotions were long considered trivial by many scientists. Lacking anything like a complete understanding of metabolic processes and the subtle electrochemical links between nerves and organs, those researchers who ventured to explore the territories of feeling were hard-pressed to explain why and how people experienced emotions. Until the late 16th century they could only guess at the complicated processes now known to be involved in producing emotional experience and connecting it with its bodily reverberations.

Different organs were believed to control certain moods: Happiness, it was said, arose from the heart, anger from the liver, fear from the kidneys, and so on. Even in the 17th century, René Descartes, the brilliant French philosopher and mathematician, saw the body's emotional apparatus as largely hydraulic. He proposed that a person felt angry or sad when certain

"Everyone knows what an emotion is, until asked to give a definition."

internal valves opened and released such fluids as bile and phlegm.

A century later, at the height of the industrial revolution, the hydraulic metaphor had given way to a mechanical one. The body was like a factory, scholars suggested, with the brain as overall manager. Emotions were just one of many products churned out in the course of normal operations. Not until the late 19th century did scientists begin to recognize that emotions were not incidental, but central, to the life of the mind—and even to the survival of the species.

Pioneering English evolutionist Charles Darwin set the stage for modern investigations. In 1872 he declared that all animals possessed emotions, which drove them to certain life-preserving actions. The quickening of emotion might enable a creature to escape danger by fighting or fleeing. Such feelings as anger or jealousy helped guard sexual partners or promote tighter bonds between males and females, which gave offspring a better chance of surviving.

Since Darwin's time, physiologists, anthropologists, biologists, psychologists, and others have undertaken to find out how and why humans experience emotions and physically manifest them. They have also explored the supposed universality of emotions—whether, for example, a smile means the same thing in Borneo as it

does in Boston, and how unspoken rules of various cultures dictate the ways in which people express what they feel. Much as Victorian geographers engaged in a massive enterprise to map the entire globe, 20th-century researchers have tried to see the subjective world of emotions objectively, and whole. Today the study of emotions is a growth industry that draws new recruits from the fields of sociology, philosophy, and history, all of whom bring their own perspectives to a facet of human existence that continues to stir controversy.

In scoping out the territory of human emotions, some investigators train their focus on biology; they prefer to quantify emotions by direct measurement of states of physical arousal or depression as manifested by temperature, heart rate, electrical activity in the brain, muscle tension, the conductivity of the skin, and other bodily signals. Another broad group of researchers, behaviorist in slant, maintains that feelings, while possessing both physical and psychological components, can best be understood as reactions to immediate or long-term circumstances. They hold that a person's emotional responses follow from conditioned—that is, socially

learned—behavior. Yet a third group sees emotions not as the opposite of rationality, but as a facet of it. These feelings of the mind, they contend, are modulated and steered not simply by some deep mental reflex, but by the more calculating intellect, which ultimately controls what the mind believes it is feeling.

Most investigators fall somewhere within the triangle described by these three extreme points of view, and all have a keen awareness of how difficult it is to render objectively something as inherently subjective as emotion. As one pair of researchers put it, "Everyone knows what an emotion is, until asked to give a definition."

In English alone, there are more than 400 words assigned to emotions and sentiments, and the differences between them can be subtle indeed. Still, the differences are there: Alarm is not the same as terror, apprehension not the same as fear. But resolving shades of meaning between synonyms is relatively easy compared with defining emotions in the first place. To some theorists, almost anything that manifests itself as a detectable response—that, say, makes the face light up or the mouth go dry—is an emotion.

Darwin thought that among humans there were a myriad of things that could be called emotions, including such qualities as pride and placidity.

By the early 20th century, theorists had pared the list of basic emotions down to a mere handful. Writing in 1924, pioneering American behaviorist John B. Watson suggested that primary emotions, like primary colors, numbered just three: fear, rage, and love. In the 1970s, Paul Ekman, an emotions theorist at the University of California at San Francisco, searching for what was universal among humans, set the list at six: happiness, sadness, anger, fear, disgust, and surprise. Robert Plutchik, a psychiatry professor at New York's Albert Einstein College of Medicine, upped the emotional ante to eight in 1980, adding acceptance and expectancy to Ekman's six.

Then in 1990, as if coming full circle, psychologists Kurt Fischer, Phillip Shaver, and Peter Carnochan published a paper that seemed to make all things possible once again. There were only five primary emotions, they hypothesized—two designated as positive, love and joy; and three classified as negative, anger, sadness, and fear. But, because in their view emotions were really social creations, the total number was virtually limitless.

A common technique in such analyses is to portray the abstract business of human emotions in some easily grasped graphic form. Robert Plutchik, for instance, has borrowed the metaphor of a color wheel, adapting it to create a three-dimensional shape with tinted wedges of emotion arranged in a circle and in several tiers (*pages* 14-15), each color shading into adjacent ones as emotions seem to do in humans. But one researcher's metaphor is another's oversimplification, and Plutchik's emotional color wheel has had its share of critics. Indeed, each scholar seems to have his or her own view of how the mind's feelings can best be described scientifically. As they have from the beginning, researchers continue to engage in heated discussions over such fundamental stuff as terminology. Should hostility be included as an emotion? Or interest, or shame, or pride? Are not emotions really subordinate to broader physiological states such as tension or relaxation? The study of emotions, like everything in human experience, can itself become a producer of strong, sometimes irrational feelings.

Although emotions are quintessentially creatures of the mind, modern attempts to define emotionality focused first on its bodily manifestations. In the relatively short time that any given mental experience of emotion lasts, observers have a narrow opportunity to measure corresponding physiological changes—which typically begin with a revving up or a dampening of nervous system activity.

Further measurable alterations follow. Psychologist Carroll Izard, an emotions researcher at the University of Delaware, has described two states that virtually everyone has experienced. "You can probably remember times when your anger mounted and your pounding heart sent blood rushing to your face and to the muscles of action," he wrote in 1991. "This was likely accompanied by a strong urge to strike out at the instigator of your rage to release the tension from tightly drawn muscles. Recall also times when you experienced overwhelming sadness, when your body seemed strangely dense or ponderous, while your muscles remained slackened and impotent. Your face and chest may have ached, tears flowed, or were stifled with effort, as your body was racked with sobs."

The bodily aspects of other sentiments have been amply chronicled in world literature. Joy, for example, is frequently said to buoy the heart, passion to enflame the breast. Sorrow, as English poet John Milton knew, cross-feeds into anger. "My griefs not only pain me as a ling'ring disease," says Milton's agonized version of the

Plutchik's Metaphor: A Three-Dimensional Spectrum

Working in the 1950s at what is now the Massachusetts Mental Health Center in Boston, Robert Plutchik, today a professor of psychiatry at New York's Albert Einstein College of Medicine, found that the hardest aspects of emotions to define were their intensity and their purity. In his studies of patients, he noticed that emotions often flickered and mixed—sadness with disgust, for example, or anger with surprise. But he also knew that, despite such blurring, the expression of some basic emotions seemed to be common to all creatures.

When emotions were evolving in animals and humans, Plutchik postulated, they coalesced into identifiable responses used in such adaptive strategies as those of courtship, dominance, and parenting. Within the resulting emotional spectrum, Plutchik isolated a core of paired emotions that, because of the different mental, behavioral, and physiological responses they produce, appear to be opposites: joy and sadness, acceptance and disgust, fear and anger, anticipation and surprise. He also identified certain other emotions related to these eight but varying in strength and purity—just as colors vary in brightness and another property called saturation.

Based on these insights, Plutchik began in 1962 to develop a visual vocabulary that allowed him to compare emotions qualitatively. The result was his Emotions Solid (*right*), a three-dimensional structure consisting of eight groupings of so-called primary emotions arranged in tiers representing different degrees of intensity and purity.

According to Plutchik, emotions in the topmost tier exist only in their pure form, but those at lower levels can combine to create other feelings (*not illustrated here*): Experiencing fear and surprise together, for example, produces awe, while joy and fear yield guilt. Opposites such as fear and anger, however, may not blend at all, and a person experiencing both may feel emotionally pulled in two directions at once.

Anger

Annoyance

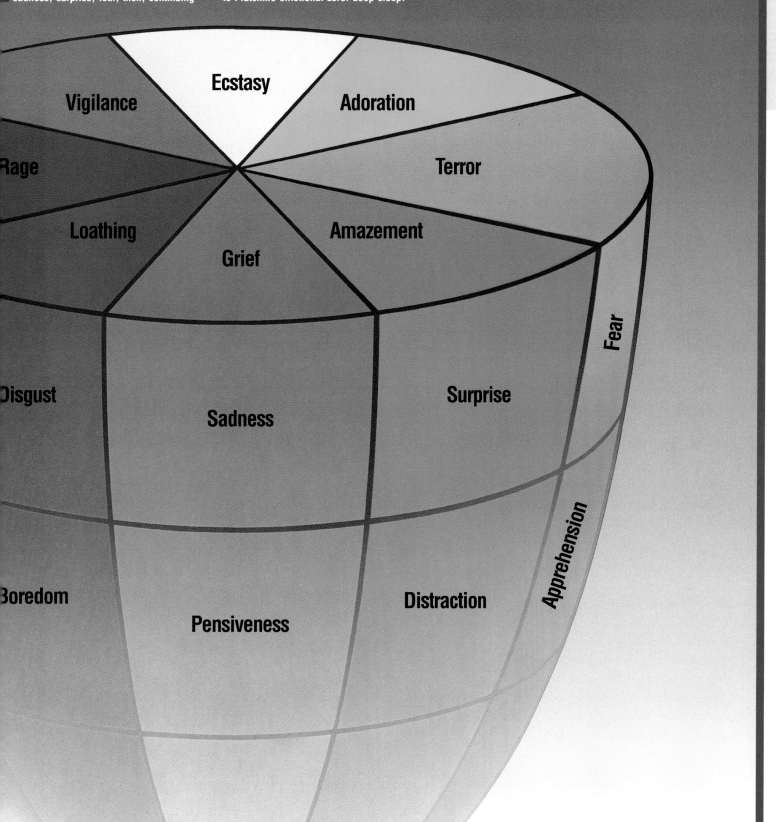

TIERS OF FEELING. Capping the Emotions Solid are the most intense and purest versions of Plutchik's eight original core emotions, which are shown on the level just below—anger, disgust, sadness, surprise, fear; then, continuing counterclockwise on the far side *(not shown)*, acceptance, joy, and anticipation. These pale into milder derivatives —sadness into pensiveness, disgust into boredom. The bottom of the Solid is Plutchik's emotional zero: deep sleep.

Ecstasy

Vigilance

Adoration

Rage

Terror

Loathing

Amazement

Grief

Disgust

Fear

Surprise

Sadness

Boredom

Apprehension

Distraction

Pensiveness

The Quest to Quantify Mood

Although the sight of an anguished child's tears evokes the same feelings in almost everyone, the language of human emotion is often too individual for useful scientific study. To quantify this elusive subject, psychologists have devised ways of measuring emotions in the lab, providing a more or less objective record of this internal, often hidden combination of physical and mental experience.

So-called psychophysiological measurements are designed to read the body's physical responses to emotional mental states. The technique typically employs electrodes to sense fluctuations in heart rate, skin conductivity, temperature, and the like—all indicative of changes in the functioning of the autonomic nervous system that may be characteristic of given emotions. Anger, for example, often causes muscles to contract involuntarily; fear makes the heart race, summons perspiration, and lowers the skin's temperature.

Psychometric scales of emotion are less objective but may produce finer detail. This method relies on the direct approach of asking people how they feel, gauging their emotional reactions to real or hypothetical situations. Sometimes the stimulus is a burning social issue. In the 1930s, for example, social scientists used questionnaires to assess people's degree of racial prejudice.

Frequently, the exploration is of a more general nature. Such is the case with experiments involving the Differential Emotions Scale, developed by psychologist Carroll Izard at the University of Delaware. In one test, subjects were asked to estimate the degree to which they experienced six basic emotional states—happiness, sadness, anger, fear, anxiety, and depression—under two different conditions: when feeling loved and when falling in love. The results suggest that when people feel loved, happiness is far and away their predominant emotion; when they fall in love, however, happiness can be accompanied by anxiety and fear—perhaps because of heightened excitement, or a troubling uncertainty about whether their feelings will be reciprocated.

biblical Samson, "but finding no redress, ferment and rage."

Scientists frequently categorize such physical echoes of emotion as either pleasurable or unpleasurable. The warmth that comes from receiving praise, the awe aroused by great works of art, the eagerness kindled by the imminent arrival of dear friends—these so-called positive sensations seem to energize the body.

Bitterness at a rival's success, sorrow over reports of the latest atrocity, or dread of failing at an assigned task all seem to carry a draining negative spiritual charge.

Such broad-stroke divisions are serviceable up to a point, providing a way to compare one type of emotional experience with another, but most investigators acknowledge that ultimately it is impossible to verify what, precisely, any person other than oneself actually senses and feels. Science falls short of being able to determine absolutely that people share the same physiological experience of anguish, anxiety, or any other emotion. Emotions may very well lie on a kind of

A PHYSICAL SIGN OF ANXIETY. In an experiment designed to explore the link between facial-muscle activity and anxiety, a tone and a red light warn this student volunteer that he is about to receive a mild electric shock. Electrodes will register even the slightest muscular twitch as he anticipates the pain.

HOW DO YOU FEEL? Results from an abbreviated Differential Emotions Scale questionnaire indicate that feeling loved brings happiness, but that falling in love leavens joy with anxiety and, to a lesser degree, fear.

Item	Happiness	Sadness	Anger	Fear	Anxiety	Depression
You feel loved.	4.78	1.28	1.13	1.19	1.57	1.19
You meet someone with whom you fall in love.	4.58	1.20	1.04	2.00	3.06	1.33

color wheel, as Robert Plutchik has proposed; but everyone's color wheel seems to be slightly different.

The true nature of an individual's passions is further camouflaged by the fact that, even in the throes of emotion, the mind appraises the situation through its lens of intellect, perhaps causing feelings to intensify or diminish. A lover's reverie may summon memories that strengthen the attachment or make affection fade. Disappointment over doing poorly on an exam may lead a student to try harder or surrender to failure. Emotions may sometimes be irrational, but they coexist with thought, reason, and memory. To a degree, cognition tells the mind what it is supposed to feel.

A set of landmark experiments conducted in 1962 illuminated the ways in which preconception and experience feed into people's assessment and labeling of their emotions. For several years, Columbia University psychologists Stanley Schachter and Jerome Singer had puzzled over how to measure the degree to which conscious evaluation plays a role in producing emotional responses. They eventually decided to take as their starting point the notion that there could be no strong emotion without an associated prior physical arousal of some kind. Accordingly, they set up an experiment in which they chemically induced a state of arousal in a group of volunteers, then exposed the subjects to certain telling stimuli.

First the volunteers, all students at the university, were divided into two groups. Members of both groups were told that they were participating in a trial of a vitamin supplement called Suproxin, ostensibly designed to improve vision; in fact, no such supplement exists. One group then received a dose of epinephrine—that is, adrenaline—to pump up the nervous system, while the other received injections of a mild saline solution that would have no effect whatever.

A third of the students dosed with epinephrine were told that they might experience minor side effects from the "supplement"—specifically, trembling hands, a flushed face, and an increased pulse, the genuine symptoms that ensue when a person's epinephrine level rises. Another third of the volunteers also heard about possible side effects, but these were spurious

ones: numbing of the feet and itching skin, neither produced by epinephrine. The final third were told nothing about possible side effects, and were left to cope with the epinephrine-induced jitters as best they could.

Now the experimenters added drama. One by one, each participant was seated in a room with a stranger as a companion, and was asked to wait 20 minutes "for the Suproxin to take effect." Unbeknown to the participants, the person in the room was not another subject, but an actor instructed by the researchers to play out one of two possible set pieces. In one scenario, the room was untidy and the actor engaged in harmless high jinks, crumpling paper and shooting it into a wastebasket, making and sailing paper airplanes, and all along chatting about how good he felt and what a great day it was. In the other scenario, the room was neat, and the actor and subject were asked to fill out long, extremely personal questionnaires designed by the researchers to bewilder and annoy. Here, the actor reluctantly cooperated for a while, commenting about the form's ridiculousness. Then, upon reaching a question regarding his sex life, he ripped up his questionnaire and exited, enraged. From

behind a one-way mirror, observers secretly watched the events unfold and noted the subjects' reactions.

The results were intriguing. Those students who had been forewarned about their bodily responses to the injection were able to look upon either the good-natured play or the histrionics of the actors without perturbation. Asked afterward how they had reacted to their companion, they reported feeling little one way or the other—that is, whatever they felt, they attributed to the side effects of the medication. But those students who had not been told to expect any response to the injection, as well as those who had been told of false symptoms, displayed a marked tendency to share the emotions being played out before them.

Thus, presented with a companion who laughed, danced, and otherwise mimed euphoria, subjects reported feeling a strong emotional uplift. Exposed to a dour, belligerent companion in a stressful setting, subjects issued angry statements or participated in aggressive actions, and later said the situation had raised their ire. As expected, the control subjects, who had been injected with saline and thus were not physiologically aroused, neither imitated the actor nor reported any feelings.

This experiment supported the idea that perception does much to shape emotions. Over the years, Schachter has grown more firm in his belief that it is only after visceral arousal that people sort out their feelings, categorize them as positive or negative, and assign them a particular name. Moreover, Schachter asserts, arousal itself is a generally undifferentiated state that can be given any label. Individuals decide what to call their emotions according to their immediate circumstances and past experiences, and according to what is on their minds at any particular moment.

According to this view, a child on her first roller-coaster ride would be physically aroused by the sensation of the earth dropping out from under her as the car plunged over the crest, but she would determine whether this arousal led to panic or pleasure by deciding whether she considered the ride safe and trusted the adult beside her. Experience would also make its contribution. Memories of having lost her balance previously—say, by tripping down the stairs—would play toward panic. If the sum of the child's associations was negative, she would tend toward fear; if positive, she would be inclined to scream with delight and come back for more.

Today, although a few scientists still consider emotions to be mainly physiological, most of them accept that emotions are the result of a complex feedback system linking biology, behavior, and cognition. Our feelings happen in the elaborate context of allegiances, beliefs, and aspirations. According to Richard Lazarus, professor emeritus of psychology at the University of California at Berkeley, emotions cannot be divorced from people's view of where they stand in the journey of their lives. Whenever a strong emotion stirs us, he writes, "the reaction tells us that an important value or goal has been engaged and is being harmed, placed at risk, or advanced. From an emotional reaction we can learn much about what a person has at stake in the encounter with the environment or in life in general, how that person interprets self

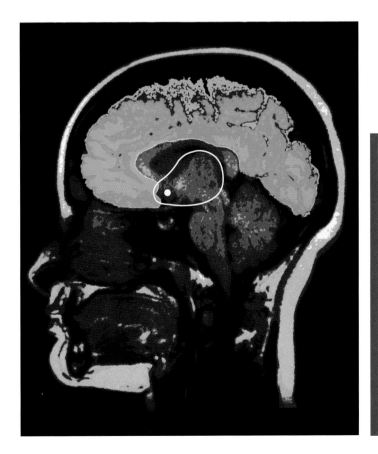

THE EMOTIONAL BRAIN. Circled in the computer-enhanced MRI brain scan at left is the location of the limbic system, a group of related components that govern the body's often involuntary responses to feelings of fear or sorrow, love or rage. Among the most important of these components is the hypothalamus *(white dot)*, which triggers the physical manifestations of emotion, such as the pounding heart and dry mouth that accompany fright. Two other limbic system elements, which come in pairs and reside in the brain's left and right hemispheres, are not visible in this midsectional scan: the amygdala, which helps to determine the appropriate behavior for a given feeling—such as crying when sad or laughing when joyful—and the hippocampus, which sees to it that very emotional incidents are remembered.

and world, and how harms, threats, and challenges are coped with."

Although emotional stirrings may be unique in terms of how each individual perceives them, they almost always translate themselves into a recognizable external signal. This may be a cringe or a shrug or some other form of body language, but more often than not it involves a facial expression—a grimace or a grin, a widening or an averting of the eyes, often a blush or a paling of the skin. Finding such manifestations relatively easy to record and analyze, scientists have a more comprehensive view of this phase of the emotional response than of any other. Indeed, some investigators suggest that feelings not expressed facially can scarcely be called emotions at all.

It is primarily by charting facial expressions worldwide and ascertaining people's interpretations of them that researchers have identified the basic emotions that appear to be standard issue for all members of the species. Some theorists have used such evidence to support the notion that the way emotions are expressed is biologically determined. But expression is also shaped by social forces.

Given that external circumstances influence emotions, it stands to reason that people from different cultures should exhibit as many differences in the expression of feelings as they do in clothing, architecture, and religious rituals. In fact, although scientists have discovered that certain basic emotions cut across cultural boundaries, and have nowhere stumbled upon people who spontaneously smile when disgusted or frown when overjoyed, they have spied many oddities in the course of international fieldwork. They have found groups who experience emotions unique to themselves and others who seem to have a peculiar inability to recognize certain emotions. The Japanese, for example, tend to have a hard time discerning anger in a face.

In addition, researchers have found that not all peoples exhibit the same emotions when confronted with similar circumstances. The death of a child, say, may elicit bitter outpourings of grief in some societies and almost no visible reaction in others. For another example, in parts of the Arab world, if a man's wife sleeps with another man it is an occasion for jealousy—not to mention punishment by death for the wife—whereas in some Inuit tribes, where men happily share their wives with friends or guests, such a response would seem absurd.

Often, variations in emotional expression are due to regulations imposed by societies upon their individual members. Around the world, elaborate calculations involving hierarchies of gender, economic class, or social standing affect where and when people are allowed to make their emotions public. The Japanese learn that in the presence of their superiors they must adopt a poker face, even when they are under duress or feel angry. In certain parts of East Asia, being in love is frowned upon, and so people bury their passion. British gentlemen were long famous for suppressing all emotional displays, and they shook their heads at the easy openness of their North American and Australian cousins.

People may go to rather extreme lengths, too, to proscribe certain emotions in one sphere while permitting them in another. Among the Utku Inuit of Canada, for instance, anger is carefully repressed. For many years, anthropologists thought that the Utku were incapable of anger because they never responded to provocations that would send most Americans into a rage. However, closer examination revealed that the Utku were redirecting their ire. The most egregious annoyance from a fellow Utku is generally deflected with humor or indifference. But, according to American anthropologist Jean Briggs, the Utku often beat and inflict other cruelties upon their dogs. Within the context of the cul-

Facial Feedback: There's a Smile That Makes Us Happy

Of all the masks that humans wear, the smile may be the most deceptive. According to Paul Ekman, of the University of California at San Francisco, there are some 18 different smiles in this repertoire—polite, cruel, false, self-effacing, and so on. But only one signifies genuine happiness.

Ekman calls that happy expression the Duchenne Smile, after 19th-century French neurologist Guillaume-Benjamin-Amand Duchenne de Boulogne, a pioneer in the study of facial expressions and emotion. Duchenne determined that the most sincerely felt smile resulted from the contraction of two muscle groups: the zygomatic muscles that pull the corners of the mouth, and the orbicularis oculi muscles, which encircle each eye. "The first obeys the will," wrote Duchenne, "but the second is only put in play by the sweet emotions of the soul."

Demonstrating the difference, Ekman puts on a stiff smile (*below, left*), then adds the crow's-feet and broader grin typical of genuine happiness (*below, right*). The first expression produces no corresponding signal within the brain. The Duchenne Smile, however, is accompanied by increased brain activity in a portion of the left hemisphere of the cerebral cortex that is associated with pleasant feelings. In what is called a facial feedback mechanism, merely putting on the Duchenne Smile produces a cerebral sensation of pleasure. Although the ensuing feeling of happiness is not as strong as that produced by a spontaneous Duchenne Smile, it may be enough to change a neutral mood into a more positive one.

ture, this avenue for venting anger is held to be acceptable, preserving the evidently necessary illusion that they are an entirely pacific people.

Each society or subculture within it, then, sets its own standards of emotional acceptability and fosters customs and institutions that reinforce those standards. But standards can alter over time. Changes in the handling of emotions can ripple through entire societies, strengthening or severing bonds between neighbors, between parents and children, and between people of different classes. Even the expression of grief has been subject to shifts in fashion.

Once, for example, American and British mourners indulged in flagrant displays of grief, staging highly stylized funerals intended, perhaps, to amplify the emotions of loss. They adhered to strict rules concerning the proper length of the mourning period and to codes dictating acceptable dress and behavior during that time. By the 1920s, however, such exaggerated habits had been dismissed as old-fashioned and grief had become muted, following a new vogue for mourning with minimal outward show. Then, during the 1980s and 1990s, another mutation occurred as the scourge of AIDS began its deadly progress across the planet. In its wake, workshops and support groups began to spring up everywhere, with coun-

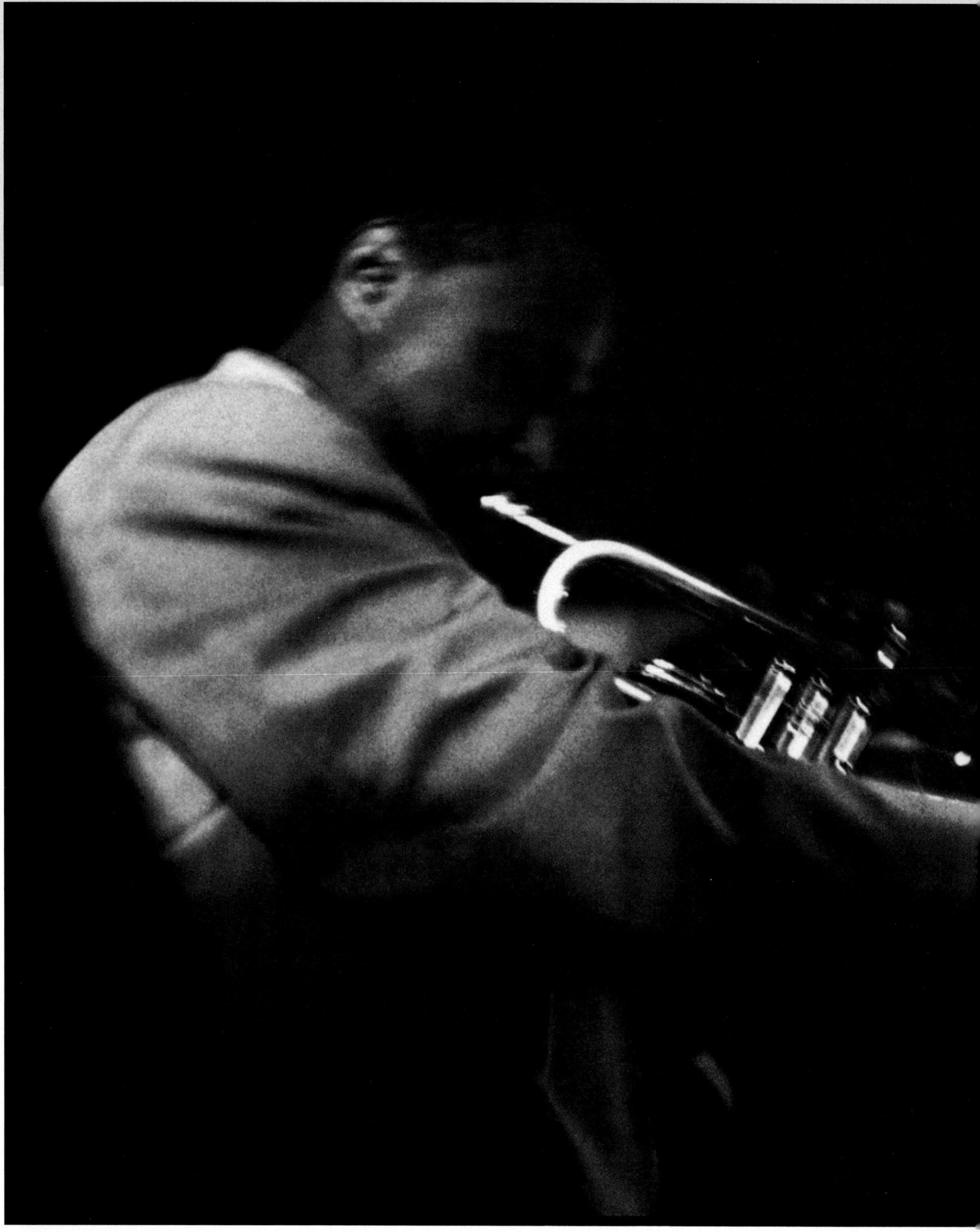

The Deep Chords that Music Strikes

All music taps the founts of human emotion, but few forms connect more directly and more purely to the feelings of the mind than the distinctive African American idiom of jazz. Itself the offspring of such deeply experienced songs as spirituals, work ballads, and the blues, jazz at its most intense has always been a medium for improvisation, a musical language set down not in notes but in moods. Anyone who hears the almost human voice of a jazz saxophone, the soaring blasts or muted wails of a trumpet, the flattened tonalities called blue notes, cannot fail to detect the human soul that haunts them.

Although jazz as an identifiable genre is a relatively recent phenomenon, such music has been with humanity from the beginning, arising from a mysterious impulse whose practical purpose is still unclear. Music exists in every culture, and it is always bound up with emotion. Indeed, the single universal feature of all music is its ability to arouse, often powerfully so. But the precise nature of the emotional arousal produced by a given combination of tones and rhythms is far from universal: One listener's cacophony may be another's lullaby. Psychologist John A. Sloboda of the University of Keele in Staffordshire, England, for example, describes feeling cheered by the upbeat rhythms and major chords of a Greek folk song, only to learn from a Greek friend that the piece was actually about desperation and despair.

People also tend to experience the physical effects of music in different ways. Some are so strongly influenced that they unconsciously regulate their breathing and heart rate to match accelerating and decelerating rhythms. This is not all that surprising, since music is registered mostly in the right hemisphere of the brain, where such autonomic functions are centered. However, like emotion itself, responses to music are a complex blending of sensations with cognition and experience. Thus, the more a person knows about a piece of music's technical elements—such as how the themes in a symphony have been developed and combined by the composer—the more likely it is that an emotive reaction will be influenced by the brain's analytically adept left hemisphere.

selors guiding survivors on how best to carry the emotional burden of a 20th-century plague.

According to many researchers, the experiencing of emotion depends not only on how we show our feelings but also on what we say about them. In this view, the language people speak actually determines partly or wholly what they are able to feel. Called the Whorf hypothesis, after American chemical engineer and amateur linguist Benjamin Whorf, this notion holds that language controls our perception of reality and thus the way we respond emotionally to it.

Each of the world's languages enables speakers to describe certain emotions easily while providing no words for discussing others. From the Whorfian perspective, for example, the Chinese appear to be splendidly equipped to describe the emotional state of shame, judging from the large number of shame-related terms in the language. There are Chinese ideograms for at least three different types of pure shame, as well as for combinations of shame and shyness, shame and resentment, shame and rage. The Chinese also consider guilt and regret as variants of shame, along with diffidence. For people whose language gives it such play, shame clearly belongs among the basic emotions.

In the Whorfian view, an abundant and precise emotional vocabulary allows emotions to be expressed more fully. Where Whorf goes wrong, according to some skeptics, is in equating this vocabulary with the ability to feel a specific emotion. Can people feel an emotion even if they have no name for it? Strict adherents of the Whorf hypothesis would say they cannot. If so, then animals are apparently incapable of experiencing emotion— a conclusion that many people find impossible to accept.

Still, it is undeniable that the language we speak affects the ease with which we conceptualize and remember emotions. For example, Germans describe the pleasure derived from the misfortune of another with the term *Schadenfreude*, literally, "harmjoy." The feeling is almost certainly universal, but they are able to express it precisely, giving the emotion greater intellectual definition.

One extensive study in the late 1970s by Oxford University social anthropologist Signe Howell revealed a strange dearth of emotional language among the Chewong, a society of hunter-gatherers living in the Malaysian rain forest. Howell spent months with these aboriginal people, becoming immersed in their language and quizzing them on their inner feelings, a task complicated by the fact that the Chewong have virtually no vocabulary for describing feelings. They have borrowed a few words from Malay that describe emotions, but their strictly indigenous terms refer only to the most basic sensations: hunger, pain, heat, cold, sexual arousal.

Despite their limited emotional vocabulary, however, Howell believes that the Chewong do in fact feel a full range of human emotions, an interpretation that runs counter to the Whorfian view. The Chewong, Howell explains, have devised "numerous and complex rules whose nature, and indeed whose very existence, demonstrate that emotions, far from being foreign to them, are of such importance as to require close control."

These rules, Howell says, are "directed towards a suppression of emotionality," and serve primarily to reinforce allegiance to the community and to foster survival amid the dangers of the jungle. There are rules to discourage a greedy hoarding of food, for example, and to limit any kind of desire that may be difficult or impossible to satisfy. One rule censors laughing at an animal, either alive or dead; another forbids "speaking badly," which means displaying any sort of emotion after an injury. To the Chewong, the language of emotion is too powerful to be left uncontained—a genie that belongs in a bottle.

Every poet, playwright, and politician shares the Chewong's special knowledge of the power of words to dampen or rouse emotion. A stirring speech or an artful play can rile an audience or soothe it, move it to tears or bring it to its feet in adulation. But the effect is rarely due to words alone. Tone of voice, music, colors, and the dance of light and shadow all strike resonant chords in human emotions.

Although precise correlations have not yet been drawn, some researchers contend that each emotional state exerts a characteristic effect on the tone of a person's voice, causing it to rise or plunge in pitch and to vary in timbre. Most people are sensitive to such vocal shifts and attribute them to specific emotions, a point not lost on great actors. In preparing for a role, Laurence Olivier would always go over his lines with great care, calibrating his utterances and memorizing them tone for tone. Such preparation, he contended, was the source of the power that marked his performances.

Certain professionals of the silver screen accord background music the same kind of obsessive attention that Olivier gave to his voice, having learned that the score can heighten an audience's emotional responses to a film. Such musical manipulations have become familiar conventions, alerting moviegoers to terror around the corner or boosting their exultation at a hero's triumph. In fact, music can fill the same bill in real life, echoing and encouraging appropriate emotional responses at weddings, football games, political rallies, and funerals. Anthony Storr, whose book *Music and the Mind* examines the powers of melody to stir the human spirit, recalls with amusement a friend whose first visit to the Grand Canyon was spoiled by the absence of a soundtrack. His friend, writes Storr, "realized that he had seen the Grand Canyon many times on the cinema screen and never without music. Because his sight of the real thing lacked such musical accompaniment, his arousal level was less intense than it had been in the cinema."

As powerful as music can be, what the eye takes in may have an even more profound effect on emotional states. Light itself plays a crucial role in regulating bodily rhythms, setting —and seasonally adjusting—daily cycles of sleeping and waking. The release of hormones, the synthesis of vitamins, and other physiological processes depend upon exposure to light. Psychologists have confirmed that the overcast days and long nights of northern winters can nudge some people into a version of depression known as seasonal affective disorder, an irregularity of mood that abates when spring arrives. Everybody likes light. Even infants respond with a gurgle of pleasure to shifting patterns of light thrown off shiny objects dangling over their cribs.

Adults placed in rooms painted in bright colors often express heightened emotional arousal and, exposed to red in any great amount, will show signs of overstimulation, including irritation and distraction, due in part to elevated blood pressure, pulse, and breathing. Blues, purples, and violets tend to soothe, while greens evoke little response. Experiments with mentally disturbed patients have revealed that colored windows casting an overall hue into a room also affect emotionality. An observer of one such test carried out in Europe in the late 19th century reported, "After passing three hours in a red room a man afflicted with taciturn delirium became gay and cheerful; on getting up the day after his entry into the room, another madman who had refused all food whatever asked for breakfast, and ate with surprising avidity."

But perhaps the most potent influence on emotions is the mind itself, which can activate feelings simply by thinking about them. Some psychologists contend that people intensify feelings of sorrow, anger, or fear by dwelling on them. The mental reiteration of feelings not only prolongs the agony but may also bring about chemical changes in the brain and body that, if they persist, can produce a full-fledged depression, rage state, or anxiety syndrome. Conversely, people who consistently remind themselves of what they like about themselves and others wind up reinforced and feeling good.

Great motivators have always known how to get people to lift their own spirits. Shakespeare has King Henry V urge his troops on to battle by exhorting them to "imitate the action of the tiger: Stiffen the sinews, summon up the blood." Henry offers a multistep program for pumping up, advising the men to "disguise fair nature with hard-favored rage; then lend the eye a terrible aspect." Through Henry, Shakespeare was acknowledging that when a person puts on a game face, the corresponding emotions often follow.

In psychological circles, this home truth is known formally as the facial feedback hypothesis, which holds that by working changes upon the muscles

Kindling Emotions with Color

As much as any other factor, the colors of an environment—a classroom, the seaside, a wallpapered kitchen—can profoundly affect the way a person feels. Not everyone experiences the same emotion in the presence of a particular color, but most people find reds and oranges stimulating and blues and purples restful. In contrast, spaces where gray, brown, black, or white dominate tend to be emotionally dulling. Indeed, a series of studies conducted in the 1970s revealed that children playing in an orange room were more friendly, alert, and creative and less irritable than children in playrooms painted white, brown, or black.

Physiological evidence adds to the picture. Red lighting, for example, has been shown to increase brain wave activity as well as blood pressure, pulse, and respiration rate. Researchers have suggested that for some deep-buried evolutionary reason, humans interpret red as the color of alarm: Bright scarlet apparently sends a signal to the brain that causes the adrenal glands to flood the body with energizing epinephrine. Strangely, pink seems to have an altogether different effect—one that is currently being put to practical use. At hundreds of correctional facilities around the world, holding cells are now painted in a bubblegum hue, officially named Baker-Miller pink, that has been found to calm angry inmates and dramatically reduce their violent behavior.

Psychologists note that people normally like most colors and tend to select primary tones when given a choice. Disturbed or unhappy people, on the other hand, often prefer neutral shades, rejecting rich colors perhaps for the very reason that they elicit unwanted or frightening emotions.

of the face, people can induce emotions in themselves. San Francisco psychologist Paul Ekman, who established a list of basic emotions in the 1970s, has done much to bolster this theory. In a series of experiments beginning in the early 1980s, he trained subjects to assume the masks of basic emotions by teaching them, muscle by muscle—some 7,000 combinations in all—how to "assemble" various expressions, without telling them which expression went with which emotion. When the subjects completed the facial flexing that corresponded to happiness, anger, fear, sadness, disgust, and surprise, a flurry of activity erupted in the nerves and organs of their autonomic nervous pathways. Most also reported experiencing the type of emotion that went with the expression they had assumed.

Ekman's work supports the notion that a stereotypical expression generates the corresponding emotion. "You can access a pleasant emotion by mechanically turning on the right facial muscle pattern," he says. In other words, people really can make themselves feel better by smiling.

But just how facial expressions influence emotional states remains an open question. Scientists know that when people assume expressions corresponding to particular emotions, their brain waves sketch signature patterns on an electroencephalogram (EEG). Further study may reveal that neuronal connections are organized in such a way that certain muscle movements trigger given emotions in the brain. Some connections may be hardwired at birth, while others are forged during the course of childhood development, when the brain's neuronal architecture is in a plastic state. This would explain why certain emotions seem to be present at birth, whereas others appear to be tailored to cultural specifications as a person matures.

Or it may turn out that the link between expressions and emotions is not quite so predetermined. Impulses from nerve sensors in the face may impinge on those portions of the brain responsible for thought and judgment, so that any message pouring in as a result of a change of expression would require some degree of higher-level interpretive processing. That would suggest that the apparent spontaneity of human emotion is just an illusion spun by the mind.

Whatever the case, all investigations of emotion to date have tended to enhance its standing in the catalog of human attributes. Almost no one today believes that emotions are merely a relic of humanity's bestial past, and few serious researchers now dismiss the mind's feelings as frivolously irrational, although they often seem to be. As psychologist Richard Lazarus has put it, emotions operate by their own intrinsic logic based on "the values, goals, and beliefs to which we are committed and which are important in our lives." When our reactions seem wrongheaded, Lazarus says, the fault more probably lies with ill-conceived commitments than with the emotions those commitments naturally evoke.

Perhaps, then, the fundamental purpose of our emotions is to guide us to our true desires, which are often camouflaged by the vagaries of experience and the chaos of daily life. "Emotions, although not themselves something that is decided upon," suggests London University philosopher Frances M. Berenson, "do illuminate our decisions on how to act and when the need to act arises. They influence our decisions about how we are to understand or see the world and the persons we come into contact with. The power which provokes real understanding here is the emotional power which illuminates and reveals to our understanding what might otherwise remain hidden." Thus, emotion is not just heat, but a bright light upon the human condition.

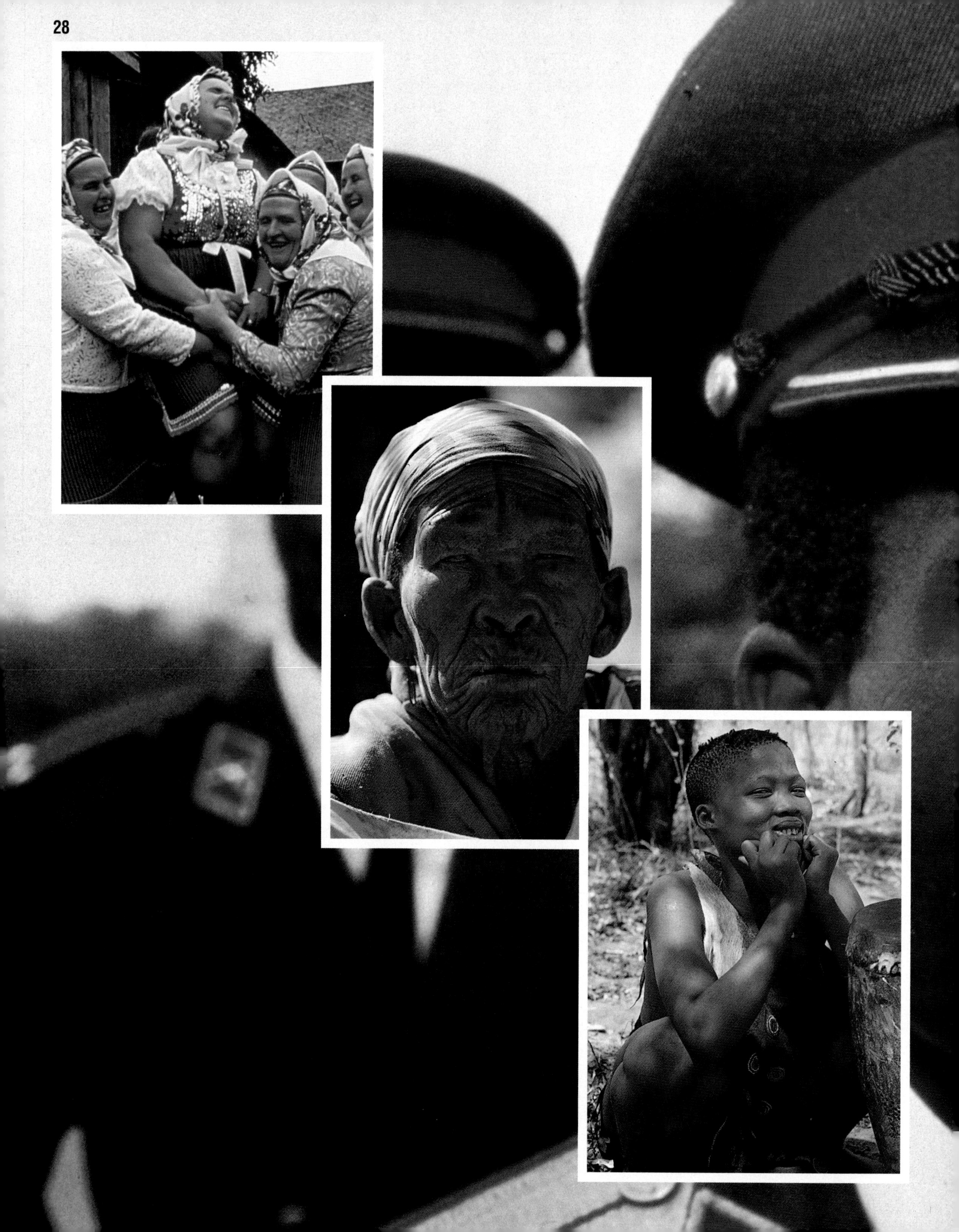

THE WIDE WORLD OF EMOTIONS

Many researchers believe that basic feelings, like primary colors, are essentially identical across cultures. Beyond the fundamentals, however, there may be as much different as there is the same about what and how people in diverse societies feel. "The effects of epinephrine may be identical in angry people from Borough Hall in Brooklyn to the beaches of Bora Bora," writes philosopher Robert Solomon, who has studied the cultural aspects of emotional experience, "but there are, nevertheless, differences in the emotional lives of various peoples, and this is where anthropology enters the picture."

Scholars have identified subtle hues on the palette of emotions that emerge only in the context of certain societies. To some researchers, these largely cultural variations illuminate the mysterious heart of human feeling, revealing the many ways in which different peoples generate, perceive, express, and manage their emotions. But these differences describe more than individual behavior. Often they define the society that creates them. On the pages that follow, anthropologists of emotion discover places where sadness is unseen, dependency is sweet, shame hides in poetry, happiness is not necessarily a good thing, and a furious goddess is a role model for humility.

LIFE WITHOUT SADNESS

"Their character," wrote German naturalist Johann Forster of Tahiti's people in 1778, "is as amiable as that of any nation that ever came unimproved out of the hands of nature." Nearly two centuries later, American anthropologist Robert Levy set out to paint a modern psychological portrait of the Polynesian islanders and found that, at least superficially, little had changed.

Levy's research may have led him to one source of the calm friendliness Forster had reported: Tahitians display emotions very differently from Westerners. Most noticeably, the Tahitian language lacks terms for sadness, longing, or loneliness. Instead, the islanders often interpret such sensations as a kind of sickness, a tendency Levy attributes to their awareness of how disturbing expressions of extreme sadness could be to their tightly bound community.

On the other hand, Tahitians can express one category of emotions that has largely vanished from the industrialized world—*mehameha*, eerie sensations felt in the presence of the supernatural. They also have an unusually large vocabulary for various forms of anger and fear. They can differentiate, for example, between the fear of something happening now and the fear of something that might happen in the future. Despite the many terms available to describe anger, however, the actual expression of that emotion is rare in Tahiti, lending credence to the notion that the more clearly people can articulate their feelings, the better they can manage them.

DEPENDENCY CAN BE SWEET

Some scholars have suggested that being able to feel an emotion depends upon having a word that describes it. The Japanese *amae* could be just such a term. Defined literally as a "sweet dependency," amae is the expectation of acceptance and care by others—the confident presumption of security that a happy child has in the presence of a loving mother.

According to Japanese psychiatrist Takeo Doi, the feeling could be universal. The fact that the word is peculiarly Japanese, however, suggests not only that the sentiment is a pervasive one in Japan, but that Japanese culture is structured to encourage its expression. As Doi wrote in his 1973 bestseller *The Anatomy of Dependence*, amae is "a key concept for the understanding not only of the psychological makeup of the individual but of the structure of Japanese society as a whole."

Psychologists Hazel Markus and Shinobu Kitayama believe that the importance of amae to the people of Japan exemplifies how emotional life is shaped by its cultural context. In community-oriented cultures like Japan's, they say, emotions that focus primarily on the individual's needs and abilities—for example, anger and pride—are downplayed. But there is a heightened sensitivity to emotions that emphasize links between people, such as amae.

The feeling may be universal, but other languages—English, for instance—offer no equivalent. When Takeo Doi explained this to a colleague, the man protested: "Why, even a puppy does it!" But only the Japanese have a word for it.

THE POETRY OF PERSONAL LIFE

While doing fieldwork among the Awlad 'Ali Bedouins of Egypt's Western Desert, American anthropologist Lila Abu-Lughod met a woman named Safiyya whose husband of 20 years had decided to divorce her. "I didn't care," Safiyya told Abu-Lughod, "I never liked him."

But two days later, while discussing her ex-husband with other women in the community, Safiyya recited a haiku-like poem—a *ghinnawa*, or "little song"—in which she expressed a very different reaction: "Memories stirred by mention of the beloved; should I release, I'd find myself flooded. . . ."

The apparent contradiction is characteristic of Awlad 'Ali emotional life. According to Abu-Lughod, men and women of the Awlad 'Ali channel their emotions into two distinct avenues of expression, one prosaic, one poetic, as part of their allegiance to the Bedouin ideal, which values autonomy above all else. To foster an image of invulnerable independence, feelings of loss and hurt are expressed in public with displays of indifference, anger, or assignments of blame.

The ghinnawa provides the Awlad 'Ali a culturally acceptable haven where feelings of attachment, affection, and despair can be expressed without violating Bedouin tenets of honorable behavior. Shared only with one's intimates, the poems are more than an emotional expression. According to Abu-Lughod, they also reinforce the code of conduct. By acknowledging in their poetry both the existence of such feelings and the difficulty of suppressing them, the Awlad 'Ali indirectly call attention to the depth of their commitment to the Bedouin way.

HEARTS GUIDED BY THE GROUP

Among the people of Ifalik, a tiny atoll in Micronesia's Caroline Islands, there is no word for emotion, although there are many "about our insides." In 1977 and 1978, anthropologist Catherine Lutz developed a list of 31 key Ifalik terms describing various feelings, and asked the islanders to sort them into categories.

Lutz found that the Ifalik categorized emotions according to the situations in which they would be experienced, rather than according to similarities among the feelings themselves. As her subjects explained, "If there is gossip about me in the village, I'll feel (emotion a) and then I'll feel (emotion b)." Lutz believes that the concept of emotions on Ifalik is defined more by the relationship of individuals to events than by one's internal feelings, as in the West.

In particular, the Ifalik distinguished between emotions that reward the individual and those that are morally correct or "good," perhaps reflecting the hard reality of atoll life. Faced with limited resources and periodic destruction from typhoons, the islanders emphasize communal ties and cooperation above all else. Happiness may shine from a group of children, but individual joy can be threatening: It interferes with one's obligations to the community.

Still, the Ifalik are not without strong feelings. Among the terms associated with human error, Lutz reported, is *song*—justified anger. The anthropologist recounts that she was reprimanded for smiling at a little girl who—contrary to social rules—had danced and made funny faces at her. The appropriate response, Lutz learned, was to show *song*.

TO BITE YOUR TONGUE

To an outsider's eye, the expression on the face of the Hindu goddess Kali (*inset*) must be one of rage—indeed, the destructive deity is the embodiment of murderous wrath. Weapon-wielding arms flailing, eyes bulging, and tongue thrust forward, Kali stands with one foot planted on what appears to be a vanquished rival. But in Bhubaneswar, a temple city in eastern India, people read something else in Kali's face, and what they see, say anthropologists Usha Menon and Richard Shweder, is a powerful example of how stylized emotional expression can be bound by a cultural context.

People in Bhubaneswar recognize the scene from Hindu legend. Kali is shown treading accidentally upon her husband, Shiva, who lay down in her path in the hope of stopping one of her lethal rampages. Kali's terrible expression is actually an embarrassed grimace, the villagers say. By stepping on her husband, Kali committed a grievous violation of the social order. Even worse, she abandoned her sense of *lajya*, a term loosely translated as a mixture of shame, embarrassment, and humility.

Lajya has a positive connotation in the Oriya language; it is the means by which women are believed to keep their natural power in check, thus maintaining social harmony. Virtuous women are expected to display lajya much the way Americans show gratitude or fidelity. In Bhubaneswar, therefore, Kali's expression is presumed to reflect her sudden realization of what she has done: Here is the very face of lajya. When the women of Bhubaneswar commit similar gaffes, they mimic the goddess's expression to signify lajya—as local idiom puts it, "to bite your tongue."

2

Evolution's Legacy

Forced from a stunted tree in the Botswanan brush onto a patch of sandy, open ground, a desperate baboon flees for his life from a hunting leopard in hot pursuit only a few paces behind him. The cat easily narrows the gap between predator and prey. Soon the two are almost touching. The leopard can hear and smell the primate's terrible fear; indeed, the signals of the other's terror must saturate the cat's sensory world. Perhaps the leopard feels a kind of exultation as well: A successful hunt means food, but also the completion of another test, the domination of another creature, the exercise of huge physical strength. This has the comforting feel of an easy kill.

Suddenly, improbably, the baboon stops his flight and whirls to face the enemy, hair erect, body quivering with aggression, long canine teeth glinting dangerously, framing an outraged scream. This unexpected display of confidence is enough to make the leopard brake, his tail whipping with blood excitement. For an instant, he may reassess this little article of prey that has abruptly turned to fight him. Perhaps the new stance means that the baboon has somehow evened the odds. But then the smell of terror, of weakness, rises through the primate's thin mask of courage. The

A Gallery of Snarls and Sneers

The inquiring eye of 19th-century English naturalist Charles Darwin seems to have probed everything connected to terrestrial life. After publishing his epochal *On the Origin of Species by Means of Natural Selection* in 1859, he continued to seek out further evidence for evolution. In 1872 he turned to the apparent similarities in the way animals and humans express certain emotions. *The Expression of the Emotions in Man and Animals* was a compendium of facial displays drawn from researchers in England and abroad, including the pioneering facial-muscle studies of French neurologist Guillaume Duchenne. From such sources, and from his own canny observations, Darwin culled a host of telling examples, eight of which appear at right.

Darwin held that basic human emotions had arisen from the instinctive responses of "lower" animals: fear, anger, happiness, and sadness. In every culture, he argued, and in every species, the facial displays of emotion were much the same. Fear made hair bristle, whether on a cat or on a human, and caused muscles to tense and jaws to drop. Clenched teeth and furrowed brow appeared on the faces of angry chimpanzees as well as on those of angry men. The wrinkled lip of a dog's snarl lived on in the human sneer. And, universally, happiness was expressed by something like a smile.

SADNESS. A sulking chimp and a pouting child share a folding of the forehead and brow.

HAPPINESS. To Darwin, this Niger baboon's sly grin corresponds to the grin of a happy man.

leopard reads it—and swiftly kills.

Though it is impossible to say what passed through the minds of the players on that day in Botswana, the facial expressions of the primate, the body language of both baboon and leopard, the victim's palpable terror—all denote emotions that humans comprehend. Certainly fear is discernible in the baboon's panicked flight. Cer-

tainly there is a kind of final courage, too, that makes the primate turn and threaten, knowing the gesture is futile. The wordless dialogue between baboon and leopard is immediately intelligible to us; their evident sensations echo through human literature and experience. In the baboon's opting to stand his ground we may see Shakespeare's Macbeth having Macduff lay on—knowing that Macduff will kill him. Indeed, human emotion resonates universally, a perpetual reminder, perhaps, that today's top ani-

ANGER. A canine snarl, Darwin believed, is forerunner to this woman's disdainful sneer.

FEAR. In man or cat, fright opens the mouth, distends neck muscles, and furrows the brow.

mals were once a part of the wild, once prey. Like the brain and body in which they manifest themselves, human emotions have traveled the long evolutionary trail.

No one heard the echo of vestigial emotion more clearly than the 19th-century naturalist Charles Darwin. Once his five years aboard the HMS *Beagle* had transformed him from a middling

divinity student into the keen scientific observer who would change the world, Darwin spent his career listening for just such signals. As early as 1837, only a year ashore, Darwin foreshadowed his interest in the springs of emotion and thought he saw them in what he took to be universally recognizable facial expressions. "Seeing a dog, horse, and man yawn," he wrote in 1837, "makes one feel how all animals are built on one structure." Emotional expression, in his view, was simply further proof of another idea

that had begun to sprout in Darwin's fertile mind: the evolution of species through a process of natural selection. Species adapted, his observations suggested, or species died. Emotional expression, Darwin believed, had to be part of that adaptation.

Such sweeping generalizations were a peculiarity of Darwin's style. He possessed, in the words of modern Austrian naturalist Konrad Lorenz, an "uncanny ability to reason on the basis of hypotheses which were not only provisional and vague but also subconscious. He deduced correct consequences from facts more suspected than known, and verified both the theory and the facts by the obvious truth of the conclusion thus reached. In other words, a man like Darwin knows more than he thinks he knows."

In 1859 Darwin's facility for hypothesis found its most famous expression in *On the Origin of Species by Means of Natural Selection, or the Preservation of Favoured Races in the Struggle for Life*. This work, which would reshape completely humanity's view of itself and of other creatures, offered the novel idea that species survived by adapting to environmental changes, through a process of natural selection—what has come to be known as survival of

the fittest. It also suggested that the realms of humans and of other organisms were not separate kingdoms but a biological commonwealth of species, linked by the imperatives of survival and reproduction: descent, as Darwin called it, from a common ancestor.

The great naturalist never tired of elucidating those connections and the light they shed upon the evolutionary process itself. He saw evidence of such descent everywhere he cast his questing eye—in the way flowers adapted to pollination by insects, in the adjustments of climbing plants, in the variations among domesticated animals and plants, and in the sexual selection process. He also found evolutionary traces in the ways emotions were expressed, and he published his ideas on the subject in The Expression of the Emotions in Man and Animals. When the book appeared in 1872 it immediately provoked a controversy.

Darwin had no doubt that animals could express emotions. He found their "means of expression" written large, if not on their faces then in the movements of their ears or feet, or in the sounds they produced. In preparing to write his book on emotional expression, he drew upon his own observations but also tapped into the work of scores of others in England and around the world. In his cordial way, Darwin would relentlessly pester experts in other fields for information.

As a result, the book brims with examples, always charmingly presented if not invariably convincing.

The neighing of a horse on being reunited with a companion, said Darwin, was a sign of joy. The shaking of a porcupine's quills and vibration of its tail showed anger. Storks evinced excitement by loudly clattering their beaks. The male lion's erected mane, he said, signaled aggressive anger. Birds ruffled their feathers when angry or frightened, emotions that drove toads and frogs to enlarge themselves by inhaling air. Darwin read impatience in a horse's pawing of the ground and fear in a dog's tucked tail. He inferred that the hippopotamus, like all creatures that fight with their teeth, drew its ears back close to its head when angry. "Even insects," wrote Darwin, "express anger, terror, jealousy, and love by their stridulation."

Because animals and humans expressed similar kinds of emotions, Darwin reasoned, the common roots and functions of those emotions could be found along the path of evolution. The precursor to human laughter, he believed, could be heard among primates who, when pleased, uttered staccato sounds while vibrating their jaws or lips, drawing the corners

of their mouth back and up, wrinkling their lower eyelids, and brightening their eyes—a facial contortion that, in humans, produces a broad smile. Similarly, he traced the sneer of the human adult to the baring of fangs in wolves and dogs. Darwin thought that such expressions had begun as behavioral reactions that increased an organism's chance of survival.

Just as Darwin's theory of evolution had rattled conventional ideas of the human place in the universe, his views on the emotions now challenged the distinction, cherished since the time of Plato and Aristotle, between the so-called rational soul believed to be unique to humans and the seemingly mechanical reflexes that appeared to govern animal behavior. The emotional difference between animals and humans, in Darwin's view, was largely one of complexity.

Such emotional expressions as trembling with fear, snarling with

A British prisoner of war snarls and gestures disdainfully at German soldiers in September 1944, after his First Airborne Division was savaged in an abortive attempt to seize the Rhine bridge at Arnhem, in the Netherlands. Scientists believe snarls evolved from such animal behavior as teeth-baring and snapping.

anger, and grinning with delight, Darwin wrote, must be innate or inherited rather than learned. To verify this, he believed, one needed only to look at the young of any species—at pups, kittens, colts, or children. In his view, the telltale clue was in the similarity of behavior in young and old. A young puppy wags its tail when pleased, just as an old dog does. Similarly, a kitten arches its back and erects its hair when frightened and angry, just as an adult cat does. Humans in distress, both young and old, display a tightening of the muscles around the eyes, obliquely slanting the eyebrows. Darwin found the precursor of that expression on the faces of babies, and he believed he understood the reason for it: Crying engorges the eyes with blood and forces the muscles surrounding the eyes to contract. In adults, who tend to repress their crying, any distress causes the muscles around their eyes to tighten.

Support for the innateness of emotions was even discernible in Darwin's own children, on whom he performed gentle experiments. When his first child was just over six months old, Darwin had the boy's nurse pretend to cry. The ruse immediately caused the son's face to assume a melancholy

expression "with the corners of the mouth strongly depressed." Doubting that his child had ever seen another child or adult cry—a real possibility in the atmosphere of the Darwin family and in Victorian England—Darwin believed that "an innate feeling must have told him that the pretended crying of his nurse expressed grief; and this through the instinct of sympathy excited grief in him."

According to Konrad Lorenz, Darwin's generalizing laid the groundwork for ethology, which the Austrian naturalist has described as the biology of behavior. Darwin's observations suggested that behavioral patterns evolved just as bones, teeth, and organs did, and he saw a clear line of descent in the repertoire of all emotional expression, animal and human. Darwin's work also indicated that some of these patterns of behavior were—like the appendix and thick body hair—the vestigial remains of ancient adaptations that had outlived their original evolutionary purpose.

One of the chief forces pushing such adaptive strategies, as Darwin recognized early on, was the need to communicate one's state to others—to show enemies that one would fight, to demonstrate subordinateness, to accommodate the natural bodily responses produced by fear, anger, joy, and other emotions. Some of that sig-

naling seemed to be inborn; but much was also learned, acquired through imitation and experience. Watching his own small tribe—he fathered 10 children—Darwin noted their extraordinary ability, from a very young age, to perceive and respond to the nonverbal cues of others, particularly to their mother's. He also observed their awareness that their own emotional expressions were being monitored by others, who might respond with praise or punishment; this consciousness induced children to alter their behavior toward the favorable result.

Darwin posited that emotions, dictated by the physical attributes of the species, "serve as the first means of communication between the mother and her infant; she smiles approval, and thus encourages her child on the right path, or frowns disapproval." Furthermore, he said, adults "readily perceive sympathy in others by their expression; our sufferings are thus mitigated and our pleasures increased; and mutual good feeling is thus strengthened."

In Darwin's view, such gestural language must have descended from human ancestors who, with no well-developed spoken language, used nonverbal communication to promote the cohesiveness they needed for survival. A cat arching its back before an intruding dog sends a message useful to both parties: If the dog crowds it, the cat is ready to fight; but if the dog reads the message clearly, a fight may be averted. For cats and dogs, and for humans and other social animals, the ability to communicate internal emotional states can make the difference between peace and war.

Although flawed by his misunderstanding of heredity—he died before the acceptance of Gregor Mendel's genetic principles—Darwin's work on emotional expression has held up well. His keen insights into the evolutionary sources of emotion have shaped all subsequent approaches to the subject. Most modern researchers now also accept the existence of an evolutionary chain of emotions linking humans and animals, especially primates, and describe a process that Darwin might have found congenial.

"Natural selection," says Jared Diamond, a physiologist at the University of California at Los Angeles, "doesn't proceed in a straight line toward a distant perceived goal, in the way that an engineer consciously designs a new product. Instead, some feature that serves one function in an animal begins to serve some other function as well, gets modified as a result, and may even lose the original function. The consequence is frequent reinven-

tions of similar adaptations, and frequent losses, shifts, or even reversals of function as living things evolve."

Because of those reinventions and functional shifts, few researchers today believe that the expression of primary emotions is the same for all species, despite apparent similarities. For expressions to be identical they must, first of all, come from species with similar physiologies and be generated by the same musculature. Only humans, for instance, are known to express astonishment with mouth agape. The manifestations of irritation in amoebas, jellyfish, dogs, and humans may all have to do with overcoming obstacles and fulfilling vital needs, but they are far too different for all of them to be called anger. Nevertheless, there appear to be more similarities than differences in the way animals—especially primates—and humans express such basic emotions as anger, fear, happiness, and sadness.

One particularly telling example of emotional similarity across species has come from the work of psychologist Donald Hebb, who observed chimpanzees for periods of six to 19 years at the Yerkes Regional Primate Research Center in Atlanta, Georgia. He found, among other things, that

they exhibited the full range of human bad temper, including sulking and, perhaps most notably, the tantrum. Year-old chimpanzees would pause in the middle of their feigned choking and head-pounding fits to see how their mothers were taking it, just as human babies do. "The evidence," New Zealand psychologist Neil McNaughton concluded in 1989, echoing the view of many colleagues, "is in favour of treating humans as just another species of animal."

The difference between the views of modern researchers and Darwin, in fact, rests largely on the importance of social context. For expressions in different species to mean the same thing, scientists now believe, they must also appear in related contexts. Darwin paid little attention to the role emotions play in everyday social interactions. He made the mistake, for example, of equating the grimace seen in primates with the human smile, when, in fact, the grimace is generally used to signal subordinate status, threat, or sexual pleasure. A real monkey smile exposes the teeth inside a wide-open mouth with the corners retracted only slightly. Context is not the only difference, however. There is a key physiological one as well. The true smile in humans employs the zygomatic muscles of the cheeks; the grimace, in apes or humans, does not (*pages* 42-43).

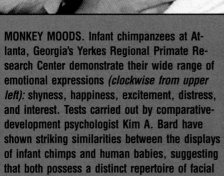

MONKEY MOODS. Infant chimpanzees at Atlanta, Georgia's Yerkes Regional Primate Research Center demonstrate their wide range of emotional expressions *(clockwise from upper left):* shyness, happiness, excitement, distress, and interest. Tests carried out by comparative-development psychologist Kim A. Bard have shown striking similarities between the displays of infant chimps and human babies, suggesting that both possess a distinct repertoire of facial expressions very early in life.

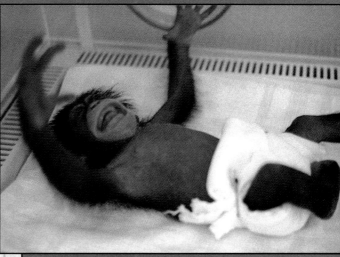

When Expressions Speak Louder Than Words

Some theorists believe that human expressions of emotion evolved primarily from various means of communication among less complex creatures. In the animal world, displays that seem to correspond to such human signals as angry scowls and happy grins convey information about an individual's emotional state. Often, however, it is more than mere social semaphore: Being understood can make the difference between life and death. Accordingly, animals use a number of channels to alert other creatures to their needs and intentions. Their repertoire includes facial and postural expressions as well as subtle changes in scent and color and a good deal of bluff. As seen in the examples here, such displays vary with situation and species, and depend greatly on what the animal brings to the act. Complex facial expressions, for example, are possible only in higher mammals that have the necessary musculature. Despite a strong resemblance between some human and animal expressions, many researchers are reluctant to attribute emotions to other species, noting that such feelings suggest a sense of self—presumed to be absent in animals.

AGGRESSIVE FISH. The raised dorsal fin of this swamp-dwelling mudskipper in Brunei is believed to be a hostile display, a declaration of territorial rights intended to warn off intruders.

FEARFUL AMPHIBIANS. In a last-ditch effort to intimidate a menacing grass snake, a threatened toad puffs up its body, using inflation as other species use bristling hair and extended feathers, to seem more formidable to predators.

BREATHLESS BIRDS. A courting male frigate bird enlarges its spectacular scarlet throat sac to attract prospective mates. The sac-inflating reflex is thought to have originated in the altered breathing patterns that accompany a stress reaction.

REPELLENT REPTILES. Jaws widened in a fearsome gape, an imperiled Australian frilled lizard heads off predators by erecting the scaly collar of skin around its neck. By splaying its frill when threatened, the arboreal insect eater can effectively double its size.

MIMING MAMMALS. Although the partially bared teeth of these sled dogs indicate aggression, the message is more complex than that. The dog on the right signals its submission by lowering its head and sticking out its tongue in a licking display that mimics the behavior of pups foraging for food.

THREE FACES OF FEAR. A trio of rhesus monkeys in the wild demonstrate how three expressions of a single emotion—in this case, fear—can serve different ends. Frightened because its mother has left it alone, the first monkey *(near right)* coos and moves around to try to regain her attention. The second monkey, alarmed by the photographer's proximity, freezes to avoid detection and attack. The third rhesus, fearful that it has been detected, glares at the intruder, bares its teeth, and barks. University of Wisconsin psychiatry professor Ned Kalin, who took these images, has studied the fear responses of both wild and captive monkeys for more than a decade. His findings have led him to conclude that the brain structures involved in fear become functional in these primates by the age of nine to 12 weeks. Other studies suggest that these structures begin functioning in humans between the ages of seven and 12 months.

Modern researchers have also elevated the communicative role of emotional expression. Although keenly aware that signaling with emotive displays was of great adaptive importance, Darwin emphasized what he called protoaction—the expressive function that indicates a readiness to act. Many studies of animals have since demonstrated that emotional displays also serve a broader evolutionary mandate by aiding such vital social interactions as sexual reproduction, declaring investments in mates and territories, and keeping relatives out of harm's way.

This evident concern for the safety of kin has been verified in a number of species. Studies of ground squirrels, for example, have shown that threatened females are more likely to sound alarm calls in the presence of their own kin. Similarly, spider monkeys lengthen the duration of their alarm calls in proportion to the number of kin in the vicinity. In the rain forests of South America, capuchin monkeys take this responsibility an extra step. When their most dreaded predator, the harpy eagle, is waiting in ambush nearby, the troop disperses and hides while the male leader struts into the open where the concealed raptor can watch his displays of interest, anger, and aggression. Though these individuals risk their lives by calling attention to themselves, they apparently accept the risk to improve their relatives' chances of survival.

Examples of such complex communication suggest that animals, like humans, are motivated by social pressures as well as by the imperatives of sheer survival. But these instances may also reveal the ancient animal sources of some human displays. The expression of interest, which most researchers group among the basic emotions, seems to offer a clear case of evolving expressive behavior. An animal attempting to see something more clearly raises the skin above its eyes, which effectively widens the eyes and increases their acuity. While this enhances the creature's ability to be interested, however, it signals nothing unless the act can be seen and read by other animals. This realization led Irenäus Eibl-Eibesfeldt, an Austrian zoologist at Germany's Max Planck Institute, to suggest in 1970 that the eyebrow evolved as a kind of flag of interest, making the brow-raising act more visible to others.

Nature is filled with adaptations that, like the primate's prominent eyebrow, seem designed to improve the clarity of the emotive message. The aggressive stare observed in a mother monkey's response to a potential attack on her infant, for example, may have the same deep evolutionary roots as the defensive glares of lizards and birds. Certain fish and insects have evolved protective spots that resemble eyes, apparently intended to deflect attacks or to draw them away from vital body parts. In India, fieldworkers wear face masks behind their heads to discourage pouncing tigers. The stare tells others one will fight, and sometimes means what it says; in the urban jungle, people who wish to avoid trouble are careful not to make strong eye contact, signaling—sometimes with a diffident smile to reinforce the message—a submissive hope of being left alone.

Because such communication has survival value, physical characteristics that increase the clarity of the signal are favored by natural selection: The

fittest of the species are those who can best express their needs and attitudes. Indeed, many theorists now believe that the complex facial musculature of all primates, including humans, evolved partly to provide unambiguous emotional displays.

While the ways in which animals and humans communicate and express emotions clearly suggest an evolutionary tie, the progression from rudimentary, bestial expressions to their complex human descendants is not clear. Indeed, the trail may have become too cold for scientists to follow. "No one can say for sure how through evolution we came to have the various emotions that we now experience," observes Carroll Izard of the University of Delaware. "We can speculate that when the first, simple forms of life emerged they had mechanisms that enabled them to respond to stimulation from the environment by accepting or rejecting, approaching or avoiding. Some emotions may have evolved from sensory processes and

physiological drives related to basic approach and avoidance behavior."

Disgust, Izard suggests, is an example. Among the first emotions a child displays, disgust is thought to have evolved from the sensory processes and physiological drives that prevented animals from eating spoiled food or drinking polluted water. It seems to appear everywhere in nature: Even viruses have been observed to make a backflip to avoid a noxious stimulus, perhaps displaying a rudimentary analogue of the disgust reflex. Human newborns, whose cerebral hemispheres are not yet fully developed, nonetheless are capable of rejecting bitter substances and of making the facial expression that signifies disgust. Then, as they grow and are exposed to a variety of foods, they will show disgust toward foods they have determined to be unpalatable. The automatic rejection evolves toward the cognitive, as memory and experience begin to shape the response.

As disgust comes under voluntary control, writes Izard, it begins to be displayed in response to things that have little to do with such objective qualities as bitterness, and a great deal to do with subjective ones—

soiled clothing, spoiled food, but also the taste of spinach, low style, foul language, other people, and even, somewhat neurotically, oneself. The biological ability to reject what is inherently repellent evolves into the largely psychological ability to be offended. Put another way, the expression of emotions not only must develop over evolutionary scales of time and across species but also must mature within individuals, where instinct is refined and altered by cognition and environment.

Evidently, this progression begins quite early in humans. According to Lois Barclay Murphy, for many years a developmental psychologist at the Menninger Foundation in Topeka, Kansas, babies begin to display distress, anxiety, joy, interest-excitement, and, sometimes, anger in the first month or two after birth. At three months or more, pleasure and delight emerge as the infants interact with the adults taking care of them; they may also display grief, fear, and distress when separated from their caregivers, responses that offer the adaptive advantage of encouraging the caregivers to remain nearby. Between seven and nine months many, though not all, infants start to show a nervousness called stranger anxiety, induced by the appearance of an unfamiliar face on their familiar scene. At nine months, some babies display signs of depression whenever the chief caretaker disappears. By the time they are a year old, human infants can express the full range of primary emotions, but complex blends such as guilt, shame, and contempt do not emerge until much later in early childhood.

While this timetable seems demonstrably correct, researchers disagree as to whether the gradual emergence of the emotions is the result of learning or of the maturation of specific portions of the nervous system. The maturation argument is supported by the precise schedule on which specific emotional expressive behaviors begin to appear. Like the appearance of buds on a tree, the process seems too rigid to be greatly influenced by the individual. A number of dramatic and inexplicable examples seem to prove the innateness of at least some basic emotional expression. For example, a 1932 study describes a 10-year-old girl who had been born deaf and blind, but who displayed pleasure by dancing and laughing, and showed resentment by turning her head, pouting, or

frowning. She could not have learned these displays by watching or listening to others. They had to be inborn.

On the other hand, few deny the enormous influence learning has on shaping and broadening such innate behavior into a full vocabulary of emotional expression. Some investigators even believe that expressions and emotions do not really connect with one another until after birth—beginning as two quite different things. Thus, in this view, the expressions are largely innate and evolve with a maturing physiology, but attaching them to their corresponding emotions must be learned.

Although the human infant's development of emotion, expression, and connections between the two suggests a kind of template of similarity from one individual to another, babies are emotionally very different and become steadily more so. As early as eight weeks, divergence can be seen: Some infants seem to have been born happy, laughing and smiling from the word go; others seem to have been irritable from birth. The difference may lie in what psychologists call temperament, often defined by emotional reactivity—the likelihood that an individual will experience basic emotions.

One of the first major investigations into temperament was begun in 1956 by New York University Medical Center psychiatrists Alexander Thomas and Stella Chess. In what they called the New York Longitudinal Study, the researchers monitored 141 New York City children for 20 years, looking for changes in nine aspects of temperament—for example, adaptability, activity level, attention span—that appeared soon after birth. In many cases, these remained relatively stable; in others, the investigators found considerable change. From their survey, Thomas and Chess were able to identify three basic patterns of temperament. The first they labeled the "easy" child—children who were usually pleasant and adapted easily to change. The second they called "difficult." These children often had irregular sleeping and eating habits and usually displayed a negative mood. The third category fell somewhere in between. Termed "slow to warm up," these children were generally less intensely negative than the difficult children, and, after being repeatedly exposed to new situations, they managed to adapt in a positive manner.

Psychologists have tended to resist the notion that temperament is inborn, concentrating instead on the importance of early experience in the development of character. But there is now compelling evidence that some behavioral traits, such as shyness, are in reality inborn ways of responding to the environment. Jerome Kagan, a professor of human development at Harvard University, has come to believe that the seeds of extreme shyness and caution are present at birth and probably lie within the genes.

The study that convinced Kagan of the biological underpinnings of shyness began in 1979. That year, he and two other psychologists, Steven Reznick and Nancy Snidman, began following the development of two very different groups of children, all about two years old. One group was extremely inhibited, the other quite easygoing and open. The researchers exposed the children to novel situations and tracked not only their behavior but also their heart rates and other physiological measures.

While the uninhibited children were largely unfazed by novelty, the shy ones displayed intense physiological responses. Their blood pressure rose, their pupils dilated, and their vocal cords tensed. Four years later the researchers found the behavioral styles of the children essentially unchanged. The shy children still showed a pattern of very inhibited behavior combined with easily excitable, revved-up nervous systems. Temperamental variables such as shyness, Kagan concluded, affect not only the ease with which emotional states are provoked but the intensity of those states as well. But this apparent biological susceptibility to shyness is not deterministic; other variables also appear to be crucial. "Nature gives the infant just a very small temperamental bias," Kagan noted in 1987. The child's "environmental context" also determines how shy he or she will be.

Innate or acquired, no emotional expression is immutable. For example, crying, the human infant's principal communicative tool, is one of nature's clearest signals of emotional condition and intensity, and the necessary apparatus is clearly inborn. While the ability to cry appears fully developed at birth, however, babies must still learn how to play this versatile instrument. According to research conducted by University of California psychiatrist Peter Ostwald and his colleagues, life teaches them quickly. The sounds made by infants only one day old apparently differ depending on whether a parent holds, bathes, or feeds the baby. Indeed, infants develop a specific hunger cry that appears to stimulate the mother's body for feeding. In one study, when 40 first-time mothers listened to a seven-minute tape of a baby's hunger cry, their breast temperature increased, a change attributed to increased milk flow. As any parent knows, a baby's hunger cry is less a lament than a call to action.

The significance of the cry, which in the beginning is just another coordinated motor pattern, changes dramatically during the first six months after birth. At first, babies cry when they are hungry or uncomfortable, and when they want attention. By their first birthday, however, the cry has begun to be attached to other experiences—petty frustration, perhaps, or fear of a stranger. Some of this is learned behavior. The one-year-old who cries over a toppled tower of blocks, for example, is taught something about emotional expression when the mother acknowledges his frustration and helps rebuild the tower. After striking his leg on a sharp corner, the same child cries in pain; the mother's concerned holding and comforting shows him that she understands his discomfort. In effect, she has labeled the feelings behind one cry as frustration, and those behind the other as pain—and taught the child that different labels elicit different maternal responses.

Crying also serves to prepare the child for speech development, providing infants with an awareness of their lips, tongue, palate, jaw, and voice. The evolution toward language, according to some investigators, is marked by shorter and shorter intervals of crying, as the interminable wail begins to assume the shorter form of syllables and words.

Like the subtler modulations of crying, the smile is not present at birth, at least not as an emotional expression. According to Harvard Medical School psychiatrist Peter Wolff, who has made extensive studies of infant emotions, expressive movements resembling a smile are quite rare in newborns while awake, but rather common during sleep. Smiles were seen, he noted, only when the infants were drowsy or sleeping. This led Wolff to conclude that the smile begins as what he called a motor release phenomenon—a spontaneous movement—that only later develops into a socially useful expression.

Once developed, the smile continues to evolve as a means of communicating emotion, changing extensively with age. Wolff found only a few one-week-old babies who smiled reliably upon hearing other humans; by the fifth week, however, all the infants in his study smiled when they heard a human voice. By eight weeks, infants were searching with their eyes for the source of the voice and smiled only after making visual contact. Then, chil-

dren two or three months old began to employ the smile very differently, using it as a response to events that seemed to serve no external, or social, function. Wolff noticed, for example, that alert infants staring at a complex geometric pattern would smile at the exact moment they stopped their inspection of the pattern. The smile seemed to indicate satisfaction.

Still, the emotions expressed by the cry and the smile appear to fulfill a larger purpose: They are the cement that binds mother and infant together. According to British psychiatrist John Bowlby and American psychologist Mary Ainsworth, whose transatlantic collaboration has endured for more than 40 years, this emotional bonding is explained by their evolutionary theory of the stages of attachment, first proposed in 1958. The theory, which has been enormously influential in the field of developmental psychology, treats the attachment of one creature to another not as a by-product of dependency, but as a means of using an emotional bond to keep someone, or something, close at hand. Thus, infant monkeys will cleave to a "mother" made of toweling, not for food but for comfort, and human infants will cry, coo, and call, wooing the mother to

give them a cuddle. Because attachment is linked to having or lacking a certain presence, it connects to such powerful emotions as love and grief, and to the motivational springs of hope and despair.

Attachment to the mother is usually a permanent bond, but infant behavior seems to confirm that the link is not forged immediately. Familial attachment appears to be at least partially an adaptation, rather than entirely innate. At birth babies display no signs of strong bonds to their families and appear oblivious to both parents and strangers. By the fourth or fifth month, however, infants have begun to respond very differently. They smile and relax at the approach of their mother; strangers get a neutral stare. By the time they are nine months old, the bond has strengthened. Infants react negatively to outsiders, but they actively focus on the mother, cooing at her, reaching for her, and crawling about the house after her. Through the unambiguous expressions of anger, frustration, hunger, and joy, the baby trains the parent to meet its myriad needs.

But this training is a reciprocal arrangement. Researchers have found that mothers generally reduce their responsiveness to such negative emotional expressions as crying when the child is about six months old, while at the same time they increase their

An Irresistible Contagion: Catching Emotions

Everyone has caught the giggles, or learned from experience that misery loves company. Emotions are as contagious as another person's yawn, compelling us to mimic the expressions, postures, and vocal cadences of those around us—indeed, to feel what we see others feeling.

The contagion strikes at birth and is never cured. A two-week-old infant mimics its parents' expressions of happiness, sadness, and fear, learning how to express emotion from their example. The image of a mother and child sharing a joyful moment illustrates the mimicry, but also demonstrates how the contagion can spread: Few people are not buoyed by the sight of others' happiness.

Just as infants sense a mother's calm, however, they also can share her anxiety. In fact, some children may contract so many negative emotions from parents that they become "insecurely attached" and may later be aggressive and lack compassion.

Emotional mimicry is rendered more subtle by experience. As we grow older, we learn, however inadvertently, to imitate the finer nuances of the expressions of others. For example, spouses have been seen to detect and imitate facial movements from their partner that are barely detectable in laboratory measurements—in a sense, reading their companion's vibes.

responses to positive expressions such as smiles and vocalizations. By age two-and-a-half, children seem to understand that angry behavior, for example, requires justification; they begin to explain why they feel the way they do. It marks the beginning of their social knowledge of emotions.

Like comedians and mimes, children learn very early that emotional expression is more than making faces and sounds: It requires a sense of timing and context, and a knowledge of the audience. By the age of two, most toddlers have begun to work this out. A typical example is the child who hurts herself while playing alone in a backyard. Her reflex is to cry, expressing pain; she briefly sobs, then stops and looks around, only to find that no one can hear her complaint. Determined to find an audience for the emotional message she wishes to send, she walks closer to the entrance door and, sensing that her mother may be within earshot, resumes crying.

Toddlers quickly discover that, effective though a piteous wail may be, as a way of communicating emotion it runs a poor second to another, uniquely human, adaptation: syntactic language. So important is language to human emotional development that it may be impossible to consider one without the other, even very early in life. By age two, according to Rutgers

Medical School researchers Michael Lewis and Linda Michaelson, children can play emotional face-making games that demonstrate an ability to produce facial expressions appropriate to the emotional occasion. For example, asked what face a fictional child would make upon receiving an ice-cream cone, they smile; asked to show the feelings of a disappointed child, they frown. This suggests that they have already linked the verbal labels of emotions with particular feelings and displays.

Other studies have shown that children as young as two-and-a-half use emotion terms appropriately not only in labeling their own states and those of others but in understanding the causes of emotion as well. One study showed that children of this age use the words "happy," "sad," "mad," and "scared" appropriately more than half the time. They also use these terms with great frequency; about half of all their statements relating cause to effect refer to emotions. Indeed, according to James Russell, a social psychologist at the University of British Columbia, some preschoolers identify emotions more clearly by words than by the corresponding facial expressions. He found that for most emo-

tions—happiness, surprise, anger, and sadness—terms and facial expressions were equally descriptive. But for fear and disgust, words conveyed the emotional message more clearly than physical displays. This led Russell to conclude that the four- to five-year-old's knowledge of the basic emotions has a much stronger verbal orientation than researchers had previously assumed.

As children acquire these communicative skills, they also begin to discover that the way in which they express emotions is not entirely their decision. The people and the culture around them also have rules for how, when, and whether emotions should be displayed. Sometimes, as a study conducted in the early 1980s suggested, these rules for displaying emotions are more important than the emotional message itself.

Researchers at Rutgers Medical School examined the developmental changes in the spontaneous use of emotional display rules in children between six and 11. The children were given a gift in a situation that required them to use one of society's truly pervasive laws: Don't look a gift horse in the mouth; act pleased with the gift, regardless. The rule is evidently intended to reward the good intentions of the giver. Not surprisingly, this kind of emotional deceit becomes easier with age. While only half the six-year-

Although Western society hates to see a grown man cry, sometimes the emotion cannot be checked. Watching soldiers march past with the flags of defeated French regiments in February 1941 overwhelms the Frenchman at left. For Cincinnati Reds baseball star Pete Rose, record-breaking hit number 4,192 brings tears and a hug for coach Tommy Helms in 1985. "The only other time I remember crying," Rose said later, "was when my father died."

olds performed the deception, more than two-thirds of those older than six did. The same experiment also uncovered an interesting gender difference, in that girls were apparently better at learning this emotional deception than boys. For both sexes, however, the ability to deceive clearly improved with age.

Another powerful statute of socialization argues against too much emotional expression in males. It is particularly specific on the subject of tears: Boys don't cry. No doubt evolved from a primitive equation of showing weakness and becoming prey, the rule has produced some odd side effects in modern society. For example, a 1992 survey conducted by Marianne La France, a psychologist at Boston University, and Yale University psychologist Mahzarin Banaji showed that mothers are less tolerant of crying in boys than in girls, suggesting that some gender differences in the way emotions are expressed by adults are instilled by mothers during the child's infancy. Thus, these researchers conclude, women grow up to be more demonstratively expressive of their emotions than men, and claim to be more emotional than men. In fact, although men's facial expression may be less demonstrative, La France and Banaji have found little physiological difference in emotional response between the two sexes.

One of the stranger demands of society, emotionally speaking, is the occasional requirement to exhibit emotions that are not felt. Display rules insist that interest be shown to an aging relative's endlessly repeated anecdotes, that the boss's jokes provoke a jolly smile, that sadness be exhibited even at a stranger's funeral. The converse is also true: Often, display rules keep felt emotions carefully hidden.

The controlled expression and suppression of emotions was demonstrated in a 1993 series of experiments by Sherri Pataki and Margaret Clark, both psychologists at Carnegie-Mellon University. In one trial, they led young, single males to believe they were about to meet a single female. Some were told she would be attractive, some that she would be plain. The researchers assumed that males expecting to meet an attractive female would be happy at the prospect, and that those expecting to meet an unattractive female would not. Indeed, that was what the two groups of males reported, at least in private. But when they were asked to report their mood in public—believing that the female would learn what they said—both groups reported being happy. The societal edicts not to judge by appearances and not to hurt other people's feelings had come into the equation. Another study by Pataki and Clark showed how feigned emotions are

sometimes used tactically. For example, they found that subjects tended to suppress their real feelings of happiness and to give a false signal of irritability as a way of bullying others into going along with some demand.

Most researchers believe that the rules governing emotional expression are learned in the same way as any other socially determined behavior—by experience and imitation. Children learn how to display grief from their parents' response to the death of a parent, for example, as well as from drama, literature, and the news. The key to this acculturation, in fact, is itself regarded as an emotion: interest. Seen in all species, interest—marked by a visible enlivening of the face and eyes, and an alertness of the body—is perhaps the first, and certainly the most frequently experienced, positive emotion. It dominates the emotional life of an infant from birth, motivating the looking, listening, vocalizing, and motor activity that are the engine of mental and physical development. Like most innate emotions, however, interest is also shaped by external forces, especially the parents. Their actions and words can either encourage or discourage their child's emotional explorations.

But interest is not just observation and mimicry. Something else is needed to explain how individuals hone emotional skills, which require that emotions are not just comprehended, but felt as well. Children are not merely watching others but are also developing an empathy that permits them to share others' feelings. Research by New York University psychologist Martin L. Hoffman suggests that children as young as two are capable of empathic behavior and can show some understanding of the emotions of others. It is not unusual, for example, to see children of this age actually holding, patting, and comforting a melancholy parent.

Young children are noticeably better at identifying the feelings appropriate to a particular situation when they feel close ties to it. Researchers Donald Hayes and Dina Casey of the University of Maine found that four- to five-year-olds are somewhat better able to recognize and remember basic emotional reactions in a television story when humans are involved than when puppets or cartoon characters are used in the same situation. In fact, the more the fictional person resembles the child in age or gender, the more clearly the child can identify the displayed emotion.

A child's understanding of emotions changes with age in ways that reflect increasing experience, cognitive development, and changing socialization pressures. Children three to four years old are usually better able to differentiate events leading to emotions like love and joy than to ones like fear and anger. Between the ages of six and nine children begin to rely less on facial expressions than on contextual cues to resolve inconsistencies in emotional situations. Until they are about seven years old, children cannot understand that two different emotions may go together, as in the temporal sequence "I was happy that I could watch TV and then mad when I had to go to bed." The simultaneous experience of very different emotional states is even harder to grasp. The idea in "I was excited about my first airplane ride but I was also a little scared" usually is not quite clear until about age nine.

As children mature, they become better at linking their inner thoughts with emotional expressions, and also more willing to do so. The difference may be that young children still rely more on situational clues to infer their own emotional state; with age, they learn that emotions can be changed from within. In a Dutch study, six- to 15-year-old children were queried about their strategies for influencing emotional states. All believed that changing situations, like calling up friends to play, would change one's emotional experience. But the older children, those 11 to 15, believed that refocusing their thoughts could also have an impact on their emotion.

The socialization of emotions does not stop with puberty, but continues into adulthood. Indeed, it may increase its influence through an entire lifetime. The emotional perspectives of adults and children are demonstrably different. For example, a 1979 study showed that the young associated unjustified punishment with sadness; adults linked it with anger. Young children associated dishonesty with anger when apprehended, but with happiness when not. Adults thought the young should fear the consequences of their actions. Like the slower modulations of species evolu-

AN UNAMBIGUOUS EXPRESSION. Free after 444 days as an Iranian hostage, Lieutenant Colonel David Roeder whoops for joy as he deplanes at an American base in Germany in January 1981. The combination of his facial expression and demonstrative gesturing—arms raised and fists pumping the air—leaves no doubt as to the emotion he must have been feeling as he realized that his ordeal was finally over.

Blueprints for Making Faces

By exploring the expressive muscula-ture of the human face, Paul Ekman, a psychologist at the University of California at San Francisco, has learned to manipulate different sets of muscles to reproduce the expressions with which humans signal six basic emotions: fear, surprise, anger, sadness, happiness, and disgust. So ingrained are these blueprints in the human psyche that Ekman has found only one society that did not recognize his expression portraits: The mountain people of southeastern New Guinea failed to distinguish between fear and surprise. Indeed, Ekman's guidelines are dependable enough that trained models, such as the one pictured at right, can reproduce the face of most emotions on demand.

Each blueprint incorporates several variations on a theme: Surprise, for example, includes questioning surprise, dumbfounded surprise, and dazed surprise; it also varies in intensity. In all, Ekman's six blueprints can be combined to express up to 33 emotional blends. People may choose different occasions to show emotion, depending on their culture and individual style. But the blueprint, according to Ekman, is always the same.

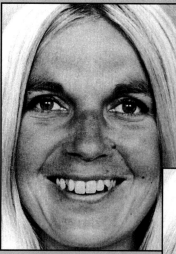

SAD EYES. Sadness brings trembling or downturned lips, triangulated upper eyelids, uplifted inner corners of the eyebrows, and raised corners of the upper eyelid.

A HAPPY FACE. Happiness is signaled by crow's-feet, wrinkles beneath the lower eyelid and between the nose and mouth, raised cheeks, raised corners of the mouth, and, sometimes, exposed teeth.

SURPRISED! A suddenly raised brow, eyes widened under stretched upper eyelids, a wrinkled forehead, and a dropped jaw form the classic recipe for the expression of surprise.

tion—the gradual transformation of snarls into sneers, for example—this process steadily alters our emotional apparatus, although most adults are not aware that it is happening at all.

No matter how elaborate the social scaffolding of emotional display, no matter whether the emotions displayed are real or feigned, the actual expressing is done mainly by the wonderfully malleable face. It is the flag that signals what we feel and the mask that hides our secret feelings. To Paul Ekman, a professor of psychology at the University of California at San Francisco, the face is also proof that,

on the whole, Charles Darwin was correct: Facial expressions of emotion are universal, biologically determined products of human evolution.

Ekman began his research in 1955 and, often working with San Francisco colleague Wallace V. Friesen, has continued it to the present. Fascinated by the marvelous fluency of the face, the two researchers have developed what Ekman calls a Facial Atlas, derived from their own observations and from the earlier work of Darwin and French neurologist Guillaume Duchenne, and from the 1931 writings of Johns Hopkins University anatomist Ernst Huber, who linked musculature and emotional expression in primates. Ekman and Friesen also drew from the more contemporary work of Robert Plutchik, whose color-wheel analogy (pages 14-

FRIGHTENED. Fear raises the upper eyelids and tenses the lower ones, draws together raised eyebrows, wrinkles the middle of the forehead, and causes tensed lips to part.

TEMPER. Vertically creased, the brow lowers and draws together over hard-staring eyes in tensed lids, and the mouth clamps shut or squared to make an angry face.

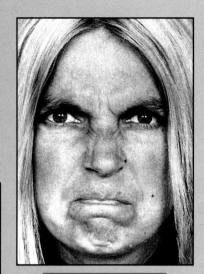

REPULSED. Raised cheeks, a wrinkled nose, lowered brow, and a lower lip either pulled up or lowered and slightly protruding show disgust.

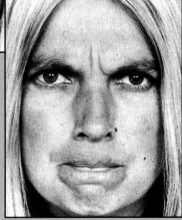

BLEND. Tight lips and tense lower eyelids combine with a raised upper lip, wrinkled nose, and elevated cheeks to indicate an emotional hybrid: anger-disgust.

15) was based on the evolutionary roots of emotion.

With those blueprints in hand, Ekman and Friesen then had professional models manipulate certain facial muscles to reproduce expressions corresponding to various emotions. They photographed the three areas of the face capable of independent motion —the brow and forehead; the eyes, eyelids, and root of the nose; and the lower face. In the Atlas, each photograph is matched with one of six primary emotions identified by Ekman. Some emotions require more detailed description than others. Surprise, for example, has one photograph each for the upper and central face, but four for the highly variable lower region.

Hoping to verify the Facial Atlas, Ekman and Friesen took their dossier of facial photographs into the field, searching for a commonality of expression among the planet's many cultures. In the course of this quest, they compiled a unique global collection of data on the faces people make, how other people read them, and how the corresponding emotion is experienced. One experiment described in the researchers' 1975 work *Unmasking the Face* compared facial expressions by student subjects in Japan and the United States. The students were shown films calculated to produce stress—scenes of a mutilating puberty rite, for example. Sometimes the subjects watched alone, sometimes with a compatriot. When the students were alone, both Japanese and Americans showed virtually identical facial expressions. "When in the presence of another person, however, where cultural rules about the management of facial appearance (display rules) would be applied," wrote Ekman and Friesen, "there was little correspondence between Japanese and American facial expressions. The Japanese masked their facial expressions of unpleasant feelings more than did the Americans." Expressions were universal, but cultural controls were not.

Showing Facial Atlas photographs to people in the United States, Japan,

Chile, Argentina, and Brazil confirmed Ekman's—and Darwin's—thesis that expressions universally represented certain primary emotions. But the researchers worried that their results might be skewed by the visual experience of global television. To see whether truly isolated peoples would recognize certain emotions expressed on the faces of aliens, they ventured into the wild highlands of southeastern New Guinea and showed modern Stone Age peoples the staged photographs of various facial expressions. The people readily identified the outward signs of grief, anger, and other emotions, although there was some confusion between fear and surprise: In the jungle the two emotions are often very close. These findings have been replicated by other researchers, including especially Carroll Izard, who asked thousands of people around the world to play a carefully designed game of "name that emotion."

Almost without exception, Ekman and Friesen found that people everywhere smile when they are happy or anticipate pleasurable feelings. When they are sad or expect unpleasantness, their faces go slack, the corners of their lips droop or tremble, they squint slightly, and their eyebrows knit together. Surprise brings a range of mouth- and eye-widening motions, and a pronounced arcing of the eyebrows. The more intense emotion of

fear, often accompanied by paleness and sweating, causes the eyebrows to rise in a straight line across the forehead, the brow to furrow, the lips to tighten, and the muscles of the lower eyelid to tense. Disgust provokes a wrinkling of the nose and a grimace.

But while the basic so-called negative emotions—anger, fear, disgust, sadness—all have a distinctive signal, according to Ekman, the family of positive emotions denoted by the term *enjoyment* do not. Amusement, relief, sensory pleasure, pride in achievement, thrill of excitement, satisfaction, and contentment are behaviorally indistinct. They are all expressed by what Ekman calls the Duchenne Smile (*page* 21). This omnibus expression is characterized not only by smiling lips but also by crow's-feet and a subtle drop of skin around the eyes. One reason the facial manifestations of positive emotions are blurred, Ekman suggests, is that, from the standpoint of survival, it may be enough to know that an emotion is positive; other details are extraneous.

In a sense, the study of the sources of emotion comes full circle with Ekman's Facial Atlas, and the various proofs he has discovered. Indeed, the San Francisco psychologist has ap-

proached emotions as a kind of modern Darwin, believing on the one hand in the evolutionary history and universality of emotions, but sharply aware on the other hand of the enormous power of learning, experience, and social imperatives.

Evolution has handed modern humans an odd mixture of such stuff. The fundamental emotional displays linked to protection, reproduction, and destruction have traveled 25 million years to reach us virtually unchanged. We still defend ourselves, reproduce, and fight. But not everything in this ancient transmission improves the human repertoire.

Nature is conservative, and the evolutionary clock is slow; we continue to receive messages from vanished worlds, and we are still moved to obey them, although their adaptive benefit was lost long ago. The machinery for raising our hackles in fear and anger lives on as goose flesh. In an age when a more cleverly adapted species would flee the sudden sound of danger, we are still inclined to stop in our tracks when startled, and, when a steady hand can make the difference between life and death, we still tremble when afraid. All of this—the rewards and penalties of complexity, the baggage that evolution piles upon descendent species—was foreshadowed a century ago. Darwin was right. He knew more than he thought he knew.

VISIBLE SIGNS OF A CHILD'S INNER WORLD

Among the many miracles of childhood, perhaps the most tantalizing is the emergence of a diverse emotional life. Parts of the process are known only approximately, because young children cannot always describe their feelings and infants are unable to talk at all. Nevertheless, researchers have managed to identify the major stages of the developmental journey. Beginning with a minimal expressive repertoire as a newborn, a child acquires such fundamental emotions as delight and apprehension within months; in later years will come such culture-shaped sentiments as guilt and shame. Meanwhile, the child learns to recognize feelings in others and to use emotions in a controlled way.

Although babies and young children are inarticulate about their inner life, they can be transparent in some respects: They lack the adult skills of regulating or concealing emotions, and the language of feeling often seems plainly written on their faces and in their gestures or postures. Children's expressions cannot always be interpreted definitively, however. The little girl above, for example, may have turned her back in anger—a simple tactic of making some irritation vanish—or she could be happily playing with a toy.

For parents and other caretakers, interpreting the feelings of children is a fascinating, never-ending pursuit. Psychologists, exploring more systematically, have found plenty of rewards of their own, as suggested by the road map of emotional growth laid out on the following pages.

A SPONTANEOUS SMILE. A newborn girl smiles in her sleep, perhaps prompted by an inner physiological state of light arousal.

A DETERMINED WAIL. One of the first and most essential forms of communication, a newborn baby's lusty cry announces his distress and helps to publicize his needs.

THE EARLIEST EMOTIONS

Although they know nothing about human interactions or the realm they have just entered, newborns display signs of certain elemental emotions. During the first hour after birth, they are often wide-eyed and alert, visibly interested as they make their first acquaintance with the world. Many parents value the postdelivery hours for creating a bond with the baby, though studies indicate that a brief separation at this time has no ill effect.

Along with expressions of interest, newborns are also quick to show distress, crying to signal their needs for food, warmth, or sleep. Disgust can appear immediately after birth, belying the romantic view of infants as little angels trailing clouds of glory. Studies reveal that, even before they have first tasted their mother's milk, newborns react to bitter liquids by turning down the corners of their mouth and pursing their lips in a frown of disapproval.

As they drift off to sleep, newborns often smile spontaneously and for no apparent reason. The experts' best guess is that such smiles appear in response to internal physiological arousal and brain activity during light sleep. Parents can evoke this so-called endogenous smile by gently stroking the baby during sleep, but it appears to be unconnected to the mother's face or to any other social event, although fond parents often offer anecdotes to the contrary. The smile's early appearance in life implies that it is innate, perhaps explaining why that particular expression is universally understood.

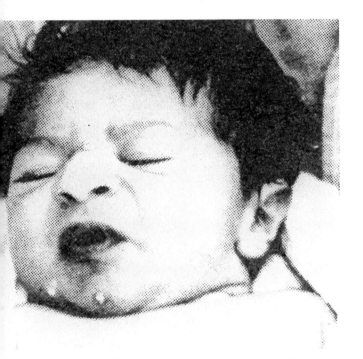

INNATE DISLIKE. Only a few hours old, a newborn rejects a bitter liquid with a frown of disgust. A sweet-tasting solution, however, is usually eagerly accepted.

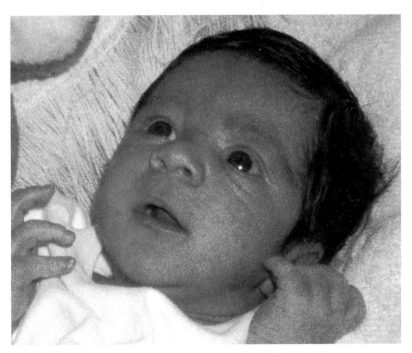

WIDE-EYED FASCINATION. With his eyebrows raised and mouth slightly open in a classic look of interest, a newborn boy gazes fixedly at a mobile hung above his crib.

THE FACE OF FURY. In an unmistakable display of anger, a girl's mouth is set in a classic squared shape and her eyebrows are forcefully drawn inward and downward.

A FEARFUL RESPONSE. A baby girl signals her apprehension by raising her eyebrows and drawing the corners of her mouth out and down.

A LOOK OF DISDAIN. Wrinkling her nose and drawing back the corners of her mouth, a little girl makes rejection crystal clear.

A RAPIDLY GROWING REPERTOIRE

During the first year of life, a baby's emotional range expands from the rudiments seen at birth to a much broader spectrum of feelings—among them, happiness, sadness, fear, anger, and surprise. These new emotions seem to develop according to a rough but fairly consistent timetable, although experts still debate when some of them emerge.

By about three months of age, babies smile consistently at social events, responding to the expressions and voices of the people around them, and after about four months, they begin to laugh. Expressions of sadness or disappointment, distinct from distress crying, also appear at this time.

Certain emotions are thought to depend on the baby's growing ability to think and remember. For example, anger usually involves recognizing a desire or goal that has been denied; the emotion typically appears between four and six months of age. When babies are about six months old, they can begin to predict the normal course of events, and they may show surprise if things fail to meet their expectations.

Fear is often the last of the emotions to appear in the first year. It emerges between seven and eight months, because, psychologists believe, this emotion involves comparing a present event with memories of the past. For example, infants must compare the face of a stranger with a remembered gallery of familiar faces before they can become frightened.

AN INQUISITIVE GAZE. His curiosity piqued, a baby boy raises his head and focuses intently on a new toy placed on his parents' bed.

A SORROWFUL GLANCE. A little boy's drooping mouth and wide, mournful eyes form the classic expression of sadness.

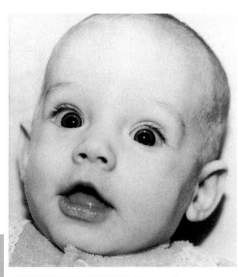

A REACTION OF SURPRISE. Her mouth agape and eyes stretched wide, a baby girl responds to the unexpected with unalloyed astonishment.

A COMFORTING ROLE. A concerned toddler runs over to her little sister and pats her on the back after hearing her cry.

PANGS OF JEALOUSY. A newly displaced middle child *(near right)* looks away, clearly disgruntled that the recent arrival has captured all of his older brother's attention.

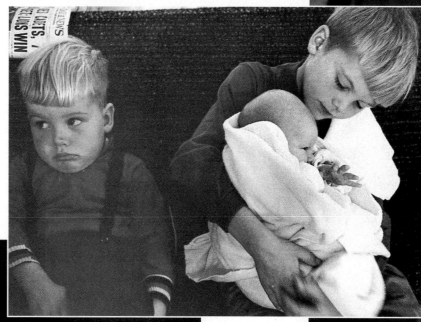

A WILLFUL TORMENTOR. Children typically express feelings of anger most openly after they have learned how their actions affect others and before they have internalized social rules.

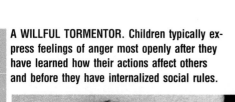

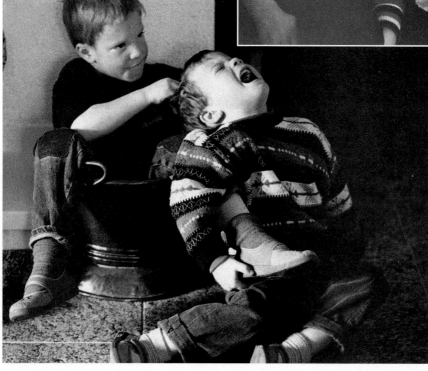

A SHY PARTYGOER. Smiling hesitantly and half averting her face, a little girl conveys her shyness—a mixture of interest and fear, attraction and apprehension.

UNDERSTANDING OTHERS

During their first year, children usually remain bystanders in emotional situations, although their mood may be influenced by feelings that they detect in a parent or other caretaker. This changes markedly as toddlers develop a sense of self-awareness during the second year of life. They begin to show empathy and insight into the feelings of others and often will comfort another child in distress, usually by hugging or patting, or by offering a beloved object such as a blanket or a stuffed animal. They may even comfort a parent: For instance, a two-year-old who sees his mother stub a toe might run over and rub it, saying, "Hurt foot."

The insight that leads children to comfort each other also teaches them how to tease or to take out their aggressive feelings on a handy target. Many children, at one time or another, vent anger on their companions—especially on younger brothers or sisters. Indeed, teasing and hurting behavior is fairly common even in children with a propensity to be sympathetic and helpful; however, those who show positive glee at the distress of others rarely exhibit any empathy.

In yet another sign of other-directed emotionality, feelings such as shyness or jealousy, which depend on comparative judgments and the perceived attitudes of other people, now begin to make their appearance. More and more, the child's sense of happiness is linked to social factors.

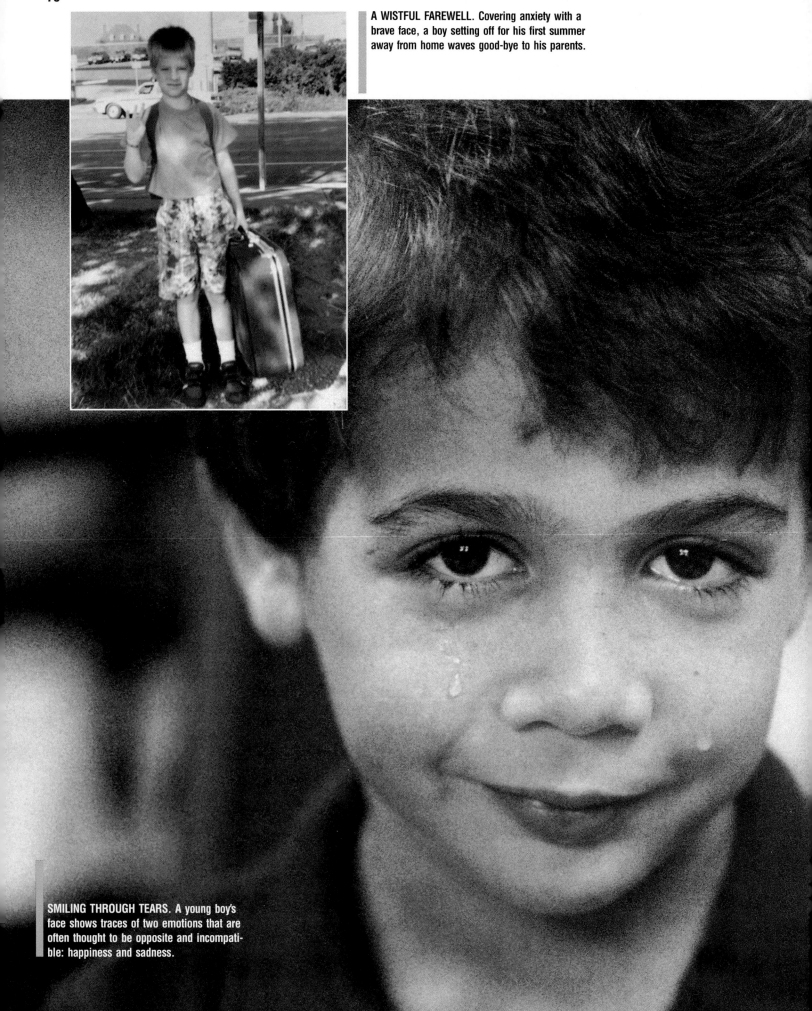

A WISTFUL FAREWELL. Covering anxiety with a brave face, a boy setting off for his first summer away from home waves good-bye to his parents.

SMILING THROUGH TEARS. A young boy's face shows traces of two emotions that are often thought to be opposite and incompatible: happiness and sadness.

A TRIUMPHANT MOMENT. Grinning broadly, a girl radiates pride and pleasure as she displays her prizewinning artwork.

A MOMENT OF RETREAT. Dealing with some unhappiness, a boy conceals his feelings by turning away and obscuring his face with a hand.

ENTERING THE SOCIAL WORLD

After children pass the milestone of their fifth birthday, they become increasingly aware of social rules and standards. Their feelings depend not only on the outcome of an event, such as obtaining a box of crayons that they want, but also on its social and moral implications—which may be very different if, for example, they receive the crayons as a gift or surreptitiously take them from a classmate.

Between the ages of six and nine, children begin to clearly associate guilt or pride with accountability. Younger children, for example, will often say that a character in a story should feel proud or guilty over something that he could not control, although the children admit that the character could not have changed what happened. Older children, by contrast, not only understand the importance of accountability but have also internalized the standards that govern these feelings; definitions that determine the meaning of an act are now stitched into their emotional life.

As children grow older, they learn rules about displaying their emotions, and they hide feelings of hurt or fear to avoid being laughed at or teased. By the time they approach the end of their first decade of life, their emotions—visible and invisible—may mix and mingle in complex ways. Younger children will say that it is impossible to feel two emotions at the same time ("because you haven't got two heads," as one child explained to a researcher). But an older child implicitly knows that one feeling can combine with another, yielding an amalgam that is not quite the same as either.

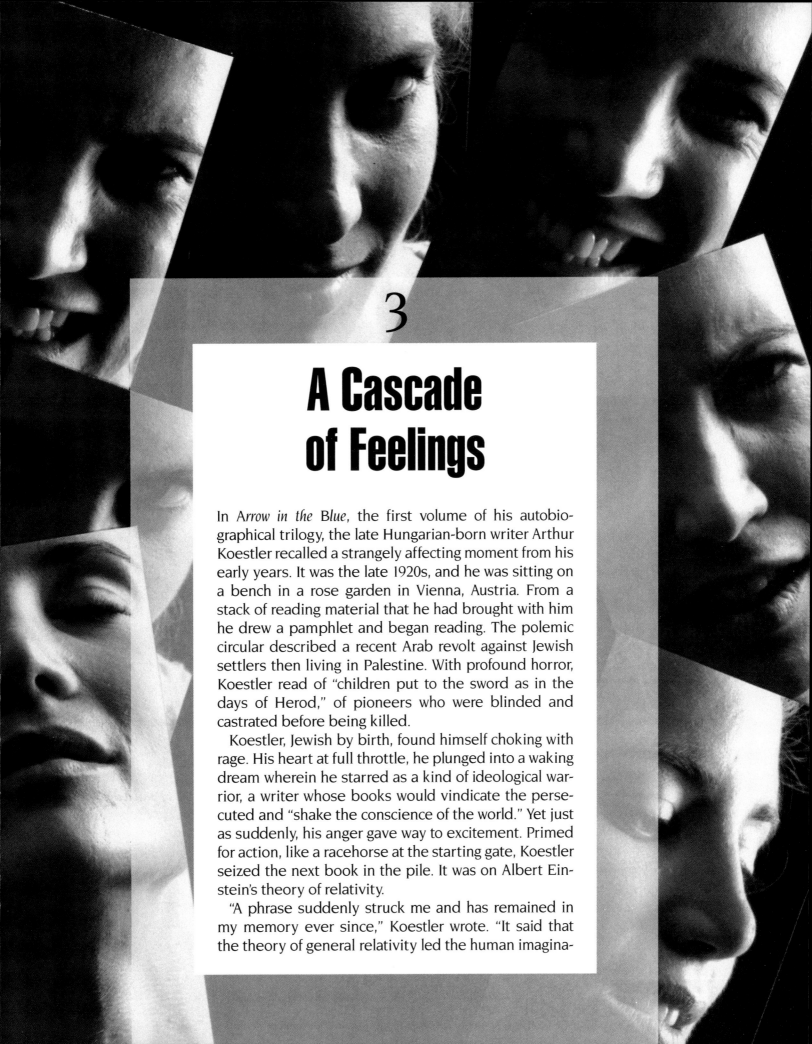

3

A Cascade of Feelings

In *Arrow in the Blue*, the first volume of his autobiographical trilogy, the late Hungarian-born writer Arthur Koestler recalled a strangely affecting moment from his early years. It was the late 1920s, and he was sitting on a bench in a rose garden in Vienna, Austria. From a stack of reading material that he had brought with him he drew a pamphlet and began reading. The polemic circular described a recent Arab revolt against Jewish settlers then living in Palestine. With profound horror, Koestler read of "children put to the sword as in the days of Herod," of pioneers who were blinded and castrated before being killed.

Koestler, Jewish by birth, found himself choking with rage. His heart at full throttle, he plunged into a waking dream wherein he starred as a kind of ideological warrior, a writer whose books would vindicate the persecuted and "shake the conscience of the world." Yet just as suddenly, his anger gave way to excitement. Primed for action, like a racehorse at the starting gate, Koestler seized the next book in the pile. It was on Albert Einstein's theory of relativity.

"A phrase suddenly struck me and has remained in my memory ever since," Koestler wrote. "It said that the theory of general relativity led the human imagination 'across the peaks of glaciers never before explored by any human being.' This cliché had an unexpectedly strong effect. I saw Einstein's world-shaking formula—Energy equals mass multiplied by the square of the velocity of light—hovering in a kind of rarefied haze over the glaciers, and this image carried a sensation of infinite tranquillity and peace." The Jewish martyrs "shrank to microscopic insignificance," Koestler said, as he came to feel that the "fate of these unfortunates had to be viewed with the same serene, detached, meditative eye as that of stars bursting into novas, of sunspots erupting, of rocks decaying into swamps, and primeval forests being transformed into coal."

With this liberating insight came a flood of new sensations. Koestler's feelings of righteous indignation and idealistic ardor were washed away—carried off, he said, by sensations of "relaxed quietude and self-dissolving stillness." In the space of a few minutes, Koestler had gone from apoplectic anger to empyreal calm.

Such is the nature of human emotion: Evanescent and mercurial, feelings roll through the psyche in never-ending waves, a boundless flux of sensations and perceptions, common to all people, yet as infinitely variable and individually precise as fingerprints. Usually they are experienced as a sort of reflex that ripples through the body and mind. We know in a general way that they are present, but we rarely give them close scrutiny; indeed, to examine each faint constellation of feeling would be to court madness. Thus the vast majority of emotions, scientists say, skitter through the gates of consciousness, perceived dimly, if at all. When we take note, as Koestler did of his successive waves of rage and tranquillity, we see the emotional landscape with unaccustomed clarity. At such moments we recognize that emotions encompass and define us. More than any other component of our psyche, perhaps, they make us human.

According to noted University of Delaware psychologist Carroll Izard, there is no thought or impression untinged by emotion—if only that of ordinary interest. Every perception is screened through an emotional lens. Indeed, as Koestler's reminiscences show, people's feelings so affect their perceptions—as well as the images and symbols attached to them—that thoughts are more properly considered emotional forces than simple ideas. Thinking of ice cream, for instance, will bring an anticipatory smile to the face of a child but may cause a weight-conscious adult to scowl at temptation. It is this sort of interplay between sentiment and reason that gives ordinary emotional experience its complex and varied form. For although most people profess to know joy, fear, love, anger, sadness—in short, the whole panoply of human emotion—there is no such thing as truly universal emotional experience. The language of emotion is slightly different for each individual.

If such diversity renders everyone's emotions unique, however, biology cuts the other way, creating a kind of physical norm that is both predictable and measurable. As neuropsychologists are discovering, certain aspects of emotion and its expression seem to be biologically predetermined—genetically hard-wired into the species, so to speak. For example, babies the world over express disgust on being fed a salty food by wrinkling the nose, curling the upper lip, and spitting out the offending substance. Similarly, the physiological response of individuals to anger is remarkably uniform across cultures and through time: The heart rate increases and blood vessels to the skeletal muscles expand; the pupils dilate to admit more light into the eyes; the bronchioles in the lungs widen as breathing deepens; and natural sugars flood the bloodstream, providing fuel for action.

The emotional offspring of cognition and biology seldom manifest them-

MIXED EMOTIONS. After the women's 200-meter final at the 1992 Olympics in Barcelona, Jamaican sprinter Grace Jackson *(far left)* seems to smile with quiet joy as she apparently comforts American Gwen Torrence, who looks almost anguished. The image shows how complex—and deceptive—emotional reactions can be. Jackson finished sixth in the race; Torrence won.

selves singly but occur as part of a complex system in which perceptions, thoughts, and a variety of attitudes interact in unpredictable ways. Small wonder, then, that scientists have found it very difficult to objectify and pinpoint emotions—to distinguish, say, between anger and fear, or annoyance and boredom—on both the experiential and neurophysiological levels. Trying to separate the two, in fact, has fueled countless experiments and psychological surveys, in which all manner of technological wizardry has been brought to bear, from computers and chemical assays to blood tests and electroencephalograms. Now, at last, researchers have begun to discern how consciousness, the unconscious mind, and biochemistry generate and shape human feelings.

One of the key findings of such research has been the idea that emotions are not individual feelings so much as a collective cascade of them. Fear, for example, is not simply being afraid of something; it also suggests prudence. Fear can debilitate, but it can also be a powerful ally, prompting an array of physiological responses to combat a threat or to escape it. Like other emotions, fear seldom exists in a pure form; rather, it is apt to be mixed with feelings of excitement, or with dejection, shame, and sadness. Oddly, however, the emotion that is

Already wounded by John W. Hinckley Jr.'s .22 pistol, President Ronald Reagan *(center)* looks toward his assailant with more interest than fear, demonstrating the close link between these often-paired emotions. Moments later, Secret Service agents thrust Reagan into his car and hurried the stricken leader out of range of the would-be assassin's gun.

most often associated with fear is interest. Some psychologists have gone so far as to suggest that fear has two indivisible faces—one characterized by the wish to flee, the other by the desire to investigate.

Austrian ethologist Konrad Lorenz offers an observation drawn from nature that illustrates this concept. One day while idly watching the sky, relates Lorenz, he spotted a raven circling above something edible on the ground—Lorenz did not say what. Keenly interested, but wary of any unfamiliar object, the raven lighted on the top branch of a tall tree to study the situation more closely, then sailed to a lower branch, focused intently on the object for a moment, and quickly returned to the higher branch. After repeating this cycle several times, the raven landed on the ground near the object and made a furtive approach. It pounced only when satisfied that its target was, as Carroll Izard has paraphrased Lorenz, "more delectable than dangerous." The same fear-interest bind marks most uncertain human explorations, as the explorer is drawn by a goal that also stimulates apprehension—the South Pole, the sound barrier, a dark alley late at night.

Fear also puts a brake on our more heedless impulses. In his American classic *The Red Badge of Courage*, 19th-century author Stephen Crane describes the sometimes macabre mix

of interest and fear elicited by the unexpected and frightening. While wandering through a thicket near a Civil War battlefield, the Union soldier Henry Fleming accidentally stumbles on the ant-covered corpse of an army comrade propped against a tree. "The youth gave a shriek as he confronted the thing," wrote Crane. "He was, for moments, turned to stone before it. He remained staring into the liquid-looking eyes. And, with it all, he received a subtle suggestion to touch the corpse. As he thought of his hand upon it, he shuddered profoundly." Here perverse interest battles with incapacitating fear. Momentarily the young soldier is turned "to stone"—a condition, commonly associated with extreme fear, in which victims are literally unable to move or speak.

The experience of fear is so potent that the anticipation or memory of it is often enough to arouse the emotion anew—or even to spawn a fear of feeling fear. According to a 1971 survey conducted by Carroll Izard and involving individuals from America, England, Germany, Sweden, France, Greece, and Japan, more persons dread the experience of fear than that of any other emotion, with good reason. Although fear can prompt the

adrenaline rush and related physical phenomena that fuel the well-known fight-or-flight response, it can also paralyze as it slips toward terror.

In the grip of such profound fear, humans and animals alike may suffer a range of ill effects, many of which target the body's nervous system and large muscles. Crane describes these responses when portraying Henry

Fleming's first exposure to real battle: "Into the youth's eyes there came a look that one can see in the orbs of a jaded horse. His back was quivering with nervous weakness and the muscles of his arms felt numb and blood-less. His hands, too, seemed large and awkward as if he was wearing invisible mittens. And there was a great uncertainty about his knee-joints."

In large enough doses, fear can even be fatal. While under its sway, vital organs such as the heart may become stressed to the point of failure. This, psychologists say, is the cause of many voodoo-related deaths; the vic-tims, believing they are cursed, can be literally scared to death.

The ability of fear or any other feeling to trigger an extreme response or behavior depends mostly on how intense the emotion is. By and large,

intensity is a subjective measure, based on an individual's arousal and degree of mental preoccupation in response to an emotional situation. The extent of physiological upset, as well as the strength of the urge to act, also figures in the intensity rating. In the case of fear, for instance, it usually happens that the more acute the fear, the greater the bodily upset and the more urgent the desire to run.

But the links between the strength of an emotion and the behavior it prompts are not always the obvious ones. In some relatively rare instances, people who find themselves in tragic circumstances feel little or nothing. Their nervous systems may register extreme agitation, and their minds may be intellectually fixed on the emotionally charged events, but their "hearts"—their emotional centers— remain, for a time, numb. Whatever inner agony they feel, they are powerless to express.

Such was the experience of Britain's Queen Victoria upon the sudden death of her beloved Prince Albert in December of 1861. Recalling her husband's last moments some 10 years later, Victoria wrote: "I bent over him and said to him, 'It is your little wife,' and he bowed his head. I asked him if he would give me a kiss, and he did so." Albert, holding his wife's hand, seemed to doze; then he took two or three long and final breaths and died.

"I stood up, kissed his dear heavenly forehead and called out in a bitter and agonizing cry, 'Oh! my dear Darling!' and then dropped on my knees in mute, distracted despair, unable to utter a word or shed a tear!"

Later, an officer of the British royal household, Sir Charles Phipps, wrote in a letter that "the Queen, though in an agony of grief, is perfectly collected, and shows a self control that is quite extraordinary. Alas! she has not realised her loss—and, when the full consciousness comes upon her—I tremble—but only for the depth of her grief." Her grief proved deep indeed. Victoria, who was 42 when Albert died, would become a living symbol of bereavement, wearing somber black and seeking as much seclusion as was possible for a monarch until her own death in 1901 at the age of 81.

In assessing Queen Victoria's initial reaction to her loss, Phipps intuitively recognized what psychologists have since articulated: that how deeply we feel an emotion, and how overtly we express it, depends in part on how truly we perceive the reality of the emotion-causing event. For some people—perhaps Victoria was one of them—the shock of losing a beloved companion seems to cushion for a time the starkness of the event. Moreover, this phenomenon appears to figure in extreme good fortune as well as in tragedy: If a couple wins 40 million dollars in the lottery tomorrow, they may not really experience the thrill attached to their luck until some of the crisp, new bills begin to pass through their hands.

Apart from perceived reality, one of the greatest enhancers of an emotion is another emotion—one that may even be wholly unrelated to the original feeling. Examples of such emotional spillover abound in everyday experience. Say, for instance, that a young girl has just finished watching a sad movie that leaves her in tears. As she walks out of the theater, her little brother tugs on her sleeve and makes a ridiculous face, causing her to burst into a fit of hilarity. She laughs until she cries. Never has she found that face so funny before. At the same time, the mirth somehow makes her feel more keenly the sorrow that the movie inspired.

Equally quirky is the property of some negative emotions to inspire positive ones. For example, fear stimulates in many people feelings of euphoria. A study of American paratroopers conducted during the 1960s reveals this sort of emotional interplay. Jumpers experiencing free fall for the first time reported feeling extreme fright. As they hurtled toward the ground, many screamed uncontrollably, curling their bodies forward. Their pupils dilated and their hearts

beat furiously. After landing safely, they walked around slightly dazed.

Within a few minutes, however, a surge of elation began to wash over them; they smiled broadly, became talkative, and gestured extravagantly. Among novice jumpers, the rush of exhilaration was short-lived, but experienced parachutists felt less fear during free fall and a more sustained postjump euphoria. This same pattern, of fear followed by euphoria, is reflected among recreational parachutists, who—along with mountain climbers, racecar drivers, and other daredevils—regularly seek out the psychic jolt that comes from courting fear. Indeed, it is the jolt that moves them to dare.

The peculiar link between fear and euphoria or joy is, according to Harvard psychology professor emeritus Richard Solomon, part of a grand emotional design in which any negative emotion is eventually followed up by a positive one, and vice versa. The Greek philosopher Plato was perhaps the first to observe this dynamic formally. "How strange would appear to be this thing that men call pleasure!" he wrote in his dialogue the *Phaedo*. "And how curiously it is related to what is thought to be its opposite,

pain! The two will never be found together in a man, and yet if you seek the one and obtain it, you are almost bound always to get the other as well."

Solomon maintains that we regularly encounter instances of this dynamic at work in our own lives. Who has not felt the letdown that comes after a joyous event, or the guilt pangs that follow on the heels of careless abandon, or relief and satisfaction on completing a nagging and onerous job? Whenever we experience any emotion intensely, Solomon says, we can count on feeling the opposite emotion afterward—rather like a balancing scale seeking equilibrium.

As fascinating as the studies of emotional dynamics may be, they afford investigators little insight into what distinguishes one emotion from another: the difference between anger and fear, for example, or jealousy and hate. Chief among the difficulties in making such distinctions is the fact that only very few people are sure of precisely what they are feeling at a given time. If Jane's boyfriend fails to show up on time for a date, is what she feels anger, worry, disappointment, or all of the above? If a coworker remarks that Jane's new haircut is "quite attractive, really," is the warm flush she experiences a response to a compliment, or an angry reaction to a perceived insult?

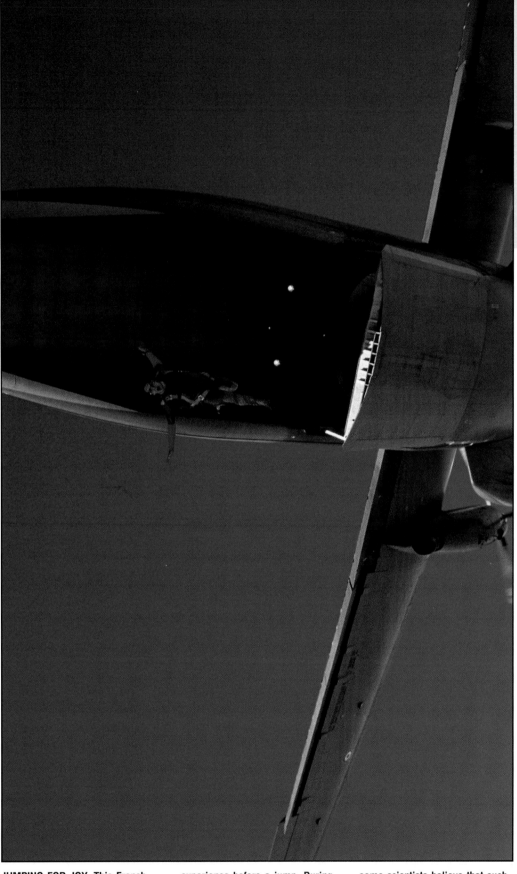

JUMPING FOR JOY. This French-man's spirited swan dive from an airborne transport's loading ramp is a sure cure, experts say, for the jitters that most parachutists experience before a jump. During the part of the jump known as free fall, fear evidently melts into a sense of euphoria that can be-come almost addictive. Indeed, some scientists believe that such chronic risk takers as sky divers are attracted to the sport mainly because it offers a heady cocktail of fear and high excitement.

Most people rely on physiological tip-offs to help them interpret what they and others are feeling. Perhaps the most readily recognized banner of feeling is the blush, which clearly denotes some kind of discomfiture, although its source can range from mild embarrassment to quivering fury. Laments one inveterate blusher, a middle-aged medical school professor, "No pumpkin in all its resplendent autumnal glory could even begin to match the glow of my face when it decides to give me away." In blush-prone individuals—and that includes nearly everyone but the very young and the severely mentally retarded—such thoughts cause the fine capillaries in the cheeks, ears, and neck to fill with bright blood. The skin grows hot and reddens, and the blusher, made doubly uncomfortable by this involuntary display, averts the gaze and turns the face away.

The blush provides undeniable evidence that certain emotions are linked with particular patterns of physiological response. Psychologist-philosopher William James in America was a pioneer in the exploration of this mind-body connection. In 1884 James proposed the radical idea that an emotion and its physiological response are not just intertwined but are, in fact, one and the same. In other words, James said, "we feel sorry because we cry, angry because we

strike, afraid because we tremble"—not the other way around. (As often seems to occur in science, another researcher, physiologist Carl Lange in Denmark, was reaching similar conclusions at about the same time and is often credited along with James as an originator of this theory.)

This is, of course, counter to the more intuitive notion that emotion stimulates bodily arousal—in effect, that we cry because we are sorry. As James saw it, some event, such as a loud noise, first triggers a physical response, such as a racing pulse. The mind then perceives the feelings generated by that response as the emotion of fear. Without this bodily arousal, James's reasoning went, no emotion would arise.

To psychologists trying to grapple with the convoluted world of emotion, James's theory was a boon that seemed on the face of it to simplify matters. If one's perception of the physiological response was in fact the emotion, then each emotion could be identified by the characteristic bodily responses associated with it.

What was plausible in theory, however, proved less straightforward in practice. A key stumbling block in the application of James's model was the

fact that a number of distinct emotions—joy, love, excitement, anger, hate, fear, jealousy, and anxiety—were found to have many physiological symptoms in common, including dizziness, trembling hands, accelerated breathing, queasy stomach, weak knees, a flushed face, and sweaty palms. If emotion was indeed equivalent to bodily response, and if several emotions shared the same arousal pattern, how did a person sort out the differences between fear and love, or excitement and joy?

In time, still more fundamental questions arose. In 1927 the American physiologist Walter Cannon put the premise of James's theory—that bodily sensations cause emotion—to an experimental test on cats. He surgically interrupted the part of the nervous system, known as the sympathetic nervous system, that helps to regulate the heart, lungs, pupils, stomach, glands, and other organs involved in emotional expression. If James was right, Cannon posited, the cats would no longer be able to experience emotion, since there was no longer circuitry from those organs to the brain.

The cats remained relatively healthy for a few months after the drastic surgery—and, Cannon discovered, they also remained emotionally active, with their ability to display feeling apparently unimpaired. When confronted with a barking dog, they still hissed, snarled, flattened their ears, bared their teeth, and lifted their paws to strike. Cannon thought his work effectively demonstrated the fallacy in James's hypothesis. His critics pointed out, however, that there was no way of knowing whether the cats actually experienced the fear they seemed to be expressing.

Studies of humans with severe spinal cord injuries have provided scientists with some possible answers to this query, although the matter is by no means resolved. In 1966 American psychologist George Hohmann, himself a paraplegic, interviewed 25 soldiers with extensive damage to the sympathetic nerves that connect the spinal cord to the internal organs. Hohmann found that in most of the men, the capacity to feel emotion had been greatly diminished. They nevertheless retained the ability to act out appropriate emotional behavior. "Now I don't get a feeling of physical animation," said one soldier, "it's sort of a cold anger. Sometimes I act angry when I see some injustice. I yell and cuss and raise hell, because if you don't do it sometimes I've learned people will take advantage of you, but it just doesn't have the heat to it that it used to. It's a mental kind of anger."

Significantly, however, four of Hohmann's informants reported no lessening of emotional intensity. And, in a more recent study of spinally injured men and women conducted in 1988, researchers encountered many individuals who professed to have passionate feelings. One man with a near-complete evisceration of his sympathetic nervous system claimed he had felt such fury at an instructor that he had wanted to "run him over a few times" with his wheelchair.

In light of these findings, James's theory would appear to have been at least partially correct. Bodily arousal does indeed seem to play a role in creating emotion, although it may not in fact cause emotion, nor even be essential to emotional experience. Cannon's hypothesis—that external events elicit emotion by exciting both the mind and the sympathetic nervous system simultaneously—is perhaps closer to the mark.

One neuroscientist who subscribes to this view is Manfred Clynes. The Austrian-born Clynes, however, takes this mind-body duet one step further: He believes that emotions, once aroused, are expressed by the brain in patterns that can be detected and used to communicate and differentiate discrete feelings—and that these patterns may arouse the very emotions they express.

To explore such interaction, Clynes,

a concert pianist who holds doctorates in both neurophysiology and engineering, has developed the "sentograph." The instrument takes its name from Clynes's designated term for the study of emotion and its expression—*sentics*, from the Latin *sentire*, "to feel." The sentograph is a rudimentary electrical device hooked up to what Clynes calls a finger rest—a device designed to sense vertical and horizontal components of pressure exerted by a subject's finger. The device feeds into a personal computer.

For more than two decades, Clynes has been putting this elegantly simple technique to work measuring, recording, and analyzing the nuances of emotional expression. By pressing the sentograph's finger rest as their feelings dictate, people are able to transmit emotion by pressure and direction in much the same way that pianists phrase music by varying their touch on the keys.

It works like this: The experimental subject sits before the sentograph and rests the middle finger of one hand on the instrument's finger rest. Clynes then instructs the person to conjure up a specific "sentic state" using mental imagery and memories to stir the appropriate feeling. Next, the

Sentics: Fingerprinting Emotion's Subtle Shapes

Proposing that emotions cause certain degrees of tension in different muscle groups, the Austrian-born neuroscientist Manfred Clynes developed a device he called the sentograph, to measure the pressure exerted by a subject's finger while a certain emotion is being experienced. Readings are plotted as a curve showing pressure variations over time. Clynes found that these curves, although generated by different people, were remarkably similar for similar emotions. Maternal or brotherly love, for example, usually generated a prolonged, smooth curve that gradually returned to the baseline. Anger, on the other hand, was marked by a sharp, sudden dip. The sentograph measures the direction of finger pressure as well as the intensity, with horizontal and vertical pressure components recorded as separate curves. According to Clynes, an angry person, for example, presses away from the body, whereas a person in love presses slightly toward the body.

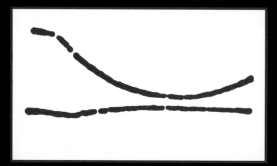

Sentograms for love *(above)* and anger *(below)* contrast sharply. The curves represent averages from 50 measurements, each taken over a two-second timespan. The upper line traces the amount of vertical pressure exerted by the subject's finger; the lower plot denotes corresponding horizontal movement either toward *(upward curve)* or away from the body.

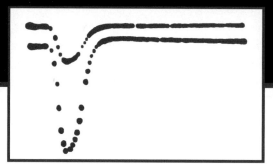

individual is asked to express the aroused emotion as precisely as possible by pressing the finger rest each time a clicking noise is heard. The finger rest converts each finger expression into an electronic signal and shunts it to the computer, which records the signal's duration and direction. When 30 to 50 expressions have been recorded for one emotion, the computer averages the data together and produces an EEG-like readout known as a sentogram.

Remarkably, sentograms for any one emotion are nearly identical, regardless of the subject's gender or culture. Love sentograms, for instance—whether they are produced by male or female, American, Japanese, Mexican, or Balinese—invariably look like a gently rolling ocean. Anger sentograms, by contrast, resemble line drawings of an earthquake zone: In each one, a daggerlike crevasse yawns menacingly between level plains. Clynes postulates that sentograms produce such distinctive but universal results because each is generated by an emotion-specific program in the brain, a program common to all people. He dubs this program the essentic form. According to Clynes, each emotion is guided and communicated by a different essentic form. Thus there is one essentic form for love that is shared by everybody, and another for anger, and so on.

Clynes suggests that what normally tends to obscure the commonality of emotion is the fact that people display their feelings in such a variety of ways: through gestures, facial expressions, music, dance, art. The sentograph, however, forces subjects to channel whatever emotion they are feeling into one communicative mode —the pressure of a finger—thereby revealing the universality of the underlying essentic forms. "We find that the essentic forms of love, anger, and grief have as great a stability as the quality of red," Clynes says.

If Manfred Clynes is right, and human emotion is driven by the psychobiological programs he calls essentic forms, then scientists may one day be able to crack the program code behind each emotion. However, investigators have yet to verify, or even agree, that such emotional software exists. Nevertheless, they are making tremendous strides in identifying what might be termed the body's emotional hardware: the parts of the brain and the neural circuits that process human emotion. Much of this progress has come from experimenting on animals, but increasingly—with the aid of new tools and imaging technologies—neuroscientists are peering directly into the human brain itself, watching as it orchestrates the complex business of feeling.

Often, the subjects who afford researchers their best glimpse into the workings of the mind are those plagued by some form of neurological disorder such as epilepsy, a condition in which the brain is periodically buffeted by electrical storms called seizures. As a rule, people with epilepsy suffer seizures in only one hemisphere of the brain. But for one woman, who has entered the annals of medicine simply as Mary, this was not the case. Starting when she was 33, Mary was troubled by mild seizures in one or the other of her cerebral hemispheres. Anticonvulsant drugs controlled the problem until she reached her fifties, when suddenly her seizures got worse. While undergoing treatment at a Canadian neuropsychiatric clinic, she began to complain of disconcerting sensations of pressure and movement in her head. Bouts of depression punctuated by flights of euphoria kept her on an emotional roller coaster. Puzzled, doctors at the clinic started monitoring Mary's brain waves with an EEG and videotaping her daily behavior.

Two patterns began to emerge. Following a right-hemisphere convulsion, manic elation overtook Mary. She danced on her bed and tried to se-

duce hospital staffers. After a seizure in her left hemisphere, however, she grew despondent and sleepless and talked of suicide.

Mary's psychiatrist began to formulate a theory: Maybe humans' positive and negative emotions are governed by separate hemispheres of the brain. Thus, when a seizure debilitates the left side, the right side's natural moroseness comes to the fore. Conversely, when a convulsion muffles the right hemisphere, the left side's unbridled high spirits charge forth.

Studies of stroke victims with injury limited to either the right or left hemisphere support this scenario. People with left-hemisphere damage are more prone to depression and gloom. Those with injuries to the right hemisphere, however, exhibit a cheerful indifference to their condition. Moreover, researchers have found that the precise location of the damage within the hemisphere profoundly influences the intensity of subsequent emotional effects. Without exception, patients with lesions in the frontal lobe of the affected hemisphere— whether right or left—exhibit the most extreme mood states.

Investigators caution that explaining these findings by labeling the left side of the brain happy and the right sad may be an oversimplification. According to neuropsychologist Don Tucker of the University of Oregon, the main emotional division of the brain may be front to back, rather than left to right. Tucker postulates that, because the frontal lobes in each hemisphere oversee human behavior as a whole, they most likely regulate emotionality too. In addition, Tucker suspects that emotional control may involve top-to-bottom coordination among the brain's various elements: The top layers regularly interact with other structures deep inside the brain that are known to affect emotions. The observed differences between the right and left hemispheres probably arise from the way each is wired to these distinct regions, he says.

The emotion-regulating structures at the core of the brain, known collectively as the limbic system, first drew attention during the early part of the 20th century. In the 1930s, while he was studying the brains of rabies victims, neuroanatomist James Papez of the Cornell Medical School in New York repeatedly found diseased tissue in one of the limbic system components—the hippocampus. This structure's proximity to the brain's oldest and most primitive region, the area surrounding the brainstem, led Papez to speculate that the hippocampus was somehow responsible for the panic and violent behavior characteristic of rabies sufferers.

Subsequent investigations began turning up evidence that other limbic

MOOD IN MOVEMENT. "Dance is a way to feel what it is to be human and to be alive," observed author Charles Fowler. Just as music and art express deep feelings directly, without the middleman of language, dance employs elements of sound, movement, pattern, form, space, shape, rhythm, time, and energy. Dance styles, although they are built on a common code, vary as widely as the emotions they communicate. In the Men's Traditional Dance of the American Plains Indians *(far right),* a colorfully costumed warrior enacts a walk through the woods, imitating birds and animals met along the way. Isadora Duncan's *Valse Brillante (near right)* exemplifies the natural movement and total freedom of expression of modern dance. The contemporary Japanese dance form known as Butoh *(above)* expresses acutely felt emotions in a diverse range of styles—from quietly spiritual to violent and chaotic. So vehement are the emotions of Butoh that the dancer often undergoes a metamorphosis during the performance, becoming another character or a figure representing a part of the earth.

structures were linked to emotion. One particularly enlightening case involved a 21-year-old epileptic named Julia. Ever since her childhood, Julia had suffered seizures that triggered panic so strong that it often caused her to run off in a frenzied trance, heedless of her destination. Her "racing spells," as she called them, often took her into dangerous neighborhoods where she would later come to her senses, shaken and afraid. She began carrying a small knife.

One evening while at the movies with her parents, Julia complained that she felt one of her spells coming

on and excused herself to go to the ladies' lounge. There she began to feel a bizarre sensation in her face and hands. Peering into the mirror, she imagined that the left side of her body had become strangely withered and evil looking. Just at that moment, another girl entered the lounge and accidentally brushed against Julia's left side. In a paroxysm of fear, Julia pulled the knife from her purse and lunged at the girl, stabbing her in the chest. Fortunately, the girl survived.

Careful monitoring of Julia's brain waves with an EEG later revealed an area of diseased tissue in her amyg- dala, a thimble-size mass of nerve fibers in the limbic system near the base of the brain. Working with the hippocampus, scientists believe, the amygdala helps generate emotions. After Julia underwent surgery to remove the amygdala, her panic attacks and violent behavior ceased.

Stories of patients like Julia underscore the importance of the limbic system in generating emotional states. But limbic structures such as the hippocampus and the amygdala cannot, by themselves, account for most human emotions. The making of an emotion is usually an immensely complex act involving many elements in the brain and nervous system, and investigators are only now beginning to isolate the neural pathways that connect the limbic system to other structures that figure in feelings.

One of the pioneers in limbic system research is Joseph LeDoux, a leading brain mapper at New York University. In 1990 LeDoux and his team of researchers embarked on a series of experiments that proved seminal in the effort to clarify how the limbic system coordinates with other parts of the brain and body in generating emotion. In the first study, investigators conditioned rats to fear a particular tone by pricking their feet with a mild electrical shock each time the tone sounded. Afterward, anytime the rodents heard the tone, they froze in fear. To learn what was going on inside the rats' brains at such times, LeDoux implanted electrodes beneath their skulls.

When the tone sounded, the electrodes traced the path of the electri-cal impulse carrying information about the noise. The signal streaked from the ear to the thalamus, a round-ish structure located just above the midbrain, the uppermost part of the brainstem. From the thalamus it raced upward toward the cerebral cortex, the convoluted rind of gray matter just under the skull that assigns meaning to sensory information. The proc-essed impulse then ricocheted down into the amygdala, whose intricate web of neurons suddenly pulsed with electrical energy.

The results seemed straightforward enough: Fearful responses were mediated first by the cortex and then by the amygdala. Not entirely satisfied with this finding, however, LeDoux conducted a follow-up experiment. After first conditioning the rats to fear the tone, he snipped the nerve circuit connecting the thalamus to the cortex. Amazingly, the surgery had no effect: The rats still froze in fear when they heard the ominous tone. Electrical monitoring of the rats' brains showed that, rather than traversing the longer route through the cortex, the impulse had taken a shortcut, shooting directly from the thalamus to the amygdala.

This unexpected outcome proved that the amygdala can trigger a fear response without input from the cere-bral cortex—in essence, that a rat can be afraid without knowing why. According to LeDoux, this happens with humans all the time. "Think of step-ping off a curb and jumping back when you suddenly hear the blast of an onrushing car's horn," he says. "You jump before you have the time to fig-ure out why. We think that's because the amygdala senses the horn before the cortex can explain it."

The brain, it appears, possesses two parallel tracks for processing emotional stimuli. In situations calling for evaluation—such as whether to feel angry or amused at the pranks of a naughty child—sensory information is routed via the thalamus to the neo-cortex, the dorsal area of the cerebral cortex. The neocortex, part of the brain's high court that governs such advanced cognitive processes as thought and language, then passes its judgment on to the amygdala. But in-formation of a simpler nature—the sight of a warm chocolate chip cookie, for instance—requires no such analy-sis. Sensory impressions of its lus-cious gooeyness bypass the cortex al-together, flashing straight from thalamus to amygdala.

Whether information arrives via the roundabout cortical route or along the more direct thalamic path, the amyg-dala must initiate the appropriate bodily response. It does this by acti-

Hormones Rush the Body toward Fight or Flight

Two simple substances, epinephrine and norepinephrine, bring the body to a state of readiness in times of stress or such extreme emotion as fear. When triggered by a threatening event, the limbic system signals the adrenal glands to secrete epinephrine and norepinephrine—also called adrenaline and noradrenaline—into the bloodstream. Circulating through the body, the hormones stimulate the fight-or-flight response. The heart rate increases, breathing becomes faster, and blood rushes to muscles and essential organs through dilated vessels. The sugar level in the blood rises to supply extra energy for the body's tissues during an emergency, and the stomach relaxes, shutting down the unnecessary activity of digestion.

The adrenal gland ordinarily secretes about four times as much epinephrine as norepinephrine, and the imbalance evidently increases when a person is frightened. Anger supposedly pushes the other way, shifting the adrenal reservoir toward a more equal blend of the two hormones. Norepinephrine is also manufactured at nerve endings of the sympathetic nervous system, where it appears to function independently of emotional surges. Like a switch activated by low blood pressure, this norepinephrine stimulates blood vessels to constrict, keeping the pressure constant.

vating nerve circuits leading to the hypothalamus, an acorn-size limbic structure located in front of and slightly below the thalamus. Besides overseeing such involuntary functions as heartbeat and body temperature, the hypothalamus also regulates hormone levels and controls sympathetic nervous system response. On a signal from the amygdala or other limbic system structure, this master regulator directs the neurons connecting the spinal cord and the body's internal organs to begin releasing the hormone epinephrine and its chemical relative, norepinephrine, from the adrenal gland above each kidney.

Together, these two chemicals produce the familiar symptoms of emotional arousal: pounding heart, trembling hands, and accelerated breathing. As one neuropsychologist put it, "Epinephrine and norepinephrine are what provide the *feeling* of a feeling: that tingle, arousal, excitement, energy." All intense emotions—love, joy, excitement, anger, fear, jealousy, and hate—provoke the same sympathetic system response, though the balance of epinephrine to norepinephrine may differ.

Epinephrine and norepinephrine are all-purpose stimulants, used to rouse the body to a general state of readiness by acting on internal organs such as the heart and lungs. But other hormones, their production prompted

Pioneers Who Linked Emotions to the Body

by the hypothalamus, have more particular effects. In fact, American psychiatrist James Henry of California's Loma Linda University postulates that numerous hormones are associated with the specific patterns of chemical and neurophysiological response that we recognize as distinct emotions. For instance, when people are depressed, Henry points out, their blood levels of the hormones adrenocorticotropin (ACTH) and cortisol rise precipitously. When they are angry, the level of norepinephrine soars, as does the level of testosterone.

Sobering evidence of testosterone's link to anger has come from the personal accounts of athletes who consume massive doses of anabolic steroids, which are synthetic analogues of testosterone. (Testosterone is primarily a male hormone; females produce it in much lower levels.) During the 1980s, South Carolina football lineman Tommy Chaikin began injecting himself with such steroids as part of a bodybuilding program. In a short time his weight climbed from 210 to 235 pounds and his muscles gained impressive mass. He also became inordinately aggressive. One evening while he was at a bar a marine bumped into Chaikin's female companion. "I saw red," Chaikin says. "I felt an aggression I'd never felt before.

I hit him so hard that he went right to the floor. I wanted to hurt him real bad. I could literally feel the hair standing up on the back of my neck, like I was a wolf or something. If I hadn't been on steroids, I would've walked away in the first place. But I had that cocky attitude. I wanted to try out my new size. I was beginning to feel like a killer."

As zoologists and other scientists have noted, sexuality and aggression are biologically linked, and, indeed, testosterone is an ingredient in the hormonal elixir that stimulates romantic love (*pages* 100-101). Also among love's chemical constituents are several naturally occurring amphetamines, including dopamine, norepinephrine, and phenylethylamine (PEA). According to psychiatrist Michael Liebowitz, the spine-tingling, toe-curling elation that accompanies infatuation is little more than a chemically induced high. Romance junkies and drug addicts have much in common, he says: Both are continually searching for the buzz that comes from exposure to these mood-altering chemicals.

But these hormones are by no means the only bodily substances

that have a major impact on emotions—nor the only ones that can behave like drugs. Also at work is a group of chemicals called neurotransmitters, which act directly on the nervous system itself, either alone or in conjunction with hormones. Neurotransmitters are naturally occurring chemicals that carry information across the infinitesimally tiny synaptic gaps that separate neurons. Some compounds, such as epinephrine and norepinephrine, do double duty, acting as hormones in the blood but as neurotransmitters in the brain.

One set of neurotransmitters, a subgroup known as endorphins, act on the brain in ways that dull pain and impart a feeling of well-being in much the same manner that morphine-based drugs do. Only since the sixties have scientists had any specific knowledge of endorphins and other neurotransmitters, although the ability of externally produced drugs to sway the emotions is common knowledge and has been for millennia. More than 6,000 years ago, the Sumerians referred to the poppy—the source of opium—as the joy plant. But the serious study of the relationship between drugs and emotional states did not begin until around the turn of the 20th century.

William James, who theorized that

WILLIAM JAMES proposed in 1884 that a reaction of the body, not the mind, triggered the conscious experience of emotion.

G. STANLEY HALL observed in an 1894 experiment that people experience a variety of physical responses to the same emotion.

WALTER CANNON reported in 1927 that cat experiments showed emotions persisting even after autonomic systems were surgically isolated.

emotion results from bodily arousal, was one of the earliest investigators of the effects of drugs on the emotions. James dosed himself with nitrous oxide, a relaxant more commonly known as laughing gas, which induced in him a giddy euphoria. He felt that he possessed eternal truths. But when the effects of the gas wore off, he could not remember his insights. One night while under the drug's influence, however, he managed to jot down the essence of one illuminating thought before lapsing into unconsciousness. The next morning he read, "Hogamus, Higamus. Man is polygamous. Higamus, Hogamus. Woman, monogamous." The drug had produced all the

emotion associated with a peak spiritual experience, but its grand world view, seen in the cold light of day, turned out to be doggerel.

If drugs can impart what seems to be authentic emotional experience, neurophysiologists reasoned, then perhaps real emotion is also chemically manufactured—albeit by the body's own natural substances. By the 1960s the widespread abuse of drugs, among them the morphine-based heroin, gave scientists an unprecedented opportunity to study the physiology behind drug-induced emotional states. Narcotics, they discovered, worked their delusive magic by docking with specialized cellular receptor sites in the brain and also in the spinal cord. That drugs could slip so easily into the body's neural receptors implied that naturally occurring

analogues of these substances were already present in the human body and might be involved in the work of regulating emotion, among other things. To find them, investigators scoured the nervous system neighborhoods targeted by the drugs, searching for chemical look-alikes. Eventually, and gradually, scientists discovered neurotransmitters. By 1987, only five of these chemicals had been isolated; today scientists have identified more than five dozen, and there may be many more to come.

The workings of these substances may be clearest in the case of one pervasive emotional state—love. The brush fire of infatuation involves the neurotransmitter dopamine, the hormone PEA, and norepinephrine, which may act as a neurotransmitter, hormone, or both. Like the addictive drugs that they resemble, PEA and its hormonal conspirators in infatuation begin to lose their punch over time. After an interval of breathless sexual attraction, the body's chemical regimen changes and—provided love lasts—morphinelike neurotransmitters known as endorphins come into play, along with the hormone oxytocin. Chemical receptors for endorphins are sprinkled throughout the limbic system and concentrated in the septum and hypothalamus, the so-called pleasure centers of the brain. The endorphins that fill these receptors are nature's tranquilizers—potent opioids that impart a profound sense of contentment.

The role of endorphins in so-called companionate love was illuminated by a study that focused on the phenomenon of separation distress—the agitation suffered by infants or young animals when they are taken from their mothers. Researchers found that when newborn puppies were given injections of the endorphin-blocking compound naloxone, their separation cries increased. Conversely, when they received small doses of an opiate beforehand, they showed fewer signs of distress on separation. As one researcher put it, it was as if the opiate was the pharmacological equivalent of the mother.

Research has shown that the emotional purview of endorphins is not limited to love. The euphoria experienced by many long-distance runners is thought to be a salutary side effect of the body's tendency to churn out endorphins during periods of stress. Not surprisingly, tests have revealed that endorphins are strongly addictive. Scientists say that the anxious, depressed feelings reported by avid runners on days they are prevented from exercising are probably due to a form of endorphin withdrawal.

Endorphins do seem to be the body's drug of choice: Apparently, even the rhapsodic joy sometimes brought on by listening to music is sparked by these natural opiates. During the 1980s, neurophysiologist Avram Goldstein of California's Stanford University performed a novel experiment designed to reveal how endorphin levels affect music appreciation. He delivered an endorphin blocker to one group of music aficionados and a placebo to another. Afterward, he treated each group to a session of its favorite music. The blocker group reported fewer chills and flights of feeling than the placebo group—

compelling evidence that endorphins fuel aesthetic sensibility.

From one perspective, biochemical models of emotion would seem to leave humankind little free will in governing its affairs: We are all, to a greater or lesser degree, at the mercy of our own inner chemistry. Indeed, psychiatrist James Henry proposes that most socially significant emotional behaviors, from friendship choices to sexual preferences to mother love, are dictated by biologically predetermined neurohormonal patterns he calls biogrammars. Henry's biogrammars are the neurophysiological equivalents of Swiss psychologist Carl Jung's archetypes—the primal, instinctive forms that Jung believed resided in the human subconscious and influenced thought and emotion.

In Henry's model, biogrammars are rooted in the lower brain structures that humans share with less evolved animals—the brainstem and limbic system—and in the class of hormones they control. Higher cortical structures have no part in these programmed emotional reflexes.

To suggest how biogrammars may take shape and subsequently direct emotional behavior, Henry cites a number of studies, among them one experiment dealing with male fetal rat development. While still in the womb, Henry notes, male rats are normally exposed to a surge of maternal tes-

It's Not How You Play the Game but Whether You Win or Lose

Everybody likes to win, and not just because it feels good. Behind every hard-won victory flows the emotional rush of a hormonal outpouring. Such chemical torrents are called biogrammars, a term coined by psychiatrist James Henry. They are predetermined endocrine patterns that guide such ancient behaviors as mating, nest building, bonding, and establishing dominance.

One human vestige of these evolutionarily ancient patterns is the hormone response that occurs with conquest. For example, tests have shown that prizewinning male tennis players had temporarily higher blood levels of testosterone than losers. Similar studies have shown that testosterone levels in men graduating from medical school also rose the day after graduation.

Such evidence has long been observed in research with animals. Male monkeys who become dominant exhibit rising levels of testosterone as long as aggressive behavior is needed to maintain their position at the top; testosterone levels fall when the monkeys lose their dominant status. But such secretions appear to increase only when the triumph is won through some kind of competitive struggle. Male lottery winners, having beaten only the odds, show no change in testosterone levels after they learn about their instant wealth.

tosterone on the 18th and 19th days of gestation. If the mother rat is stressed during this critical period, however, her testosterone levels will plummet. As a result, her developing male offspring may fail to receive their all-important jolt of hormone. The deprived rats' mating biogrammars will thus be programmed differently. When the male offspring reach maturity, they will fail to respond to female rats in a sexually appropriate manner. Although human sexuality is far more complex than that of rats, Henry also suggests that human sexual preference may be rooted in neurohormonal determinants.

Henry believes that a biogrammar also oversees the bonding that typically occurs between a mother and her newborn child. When a mother holds her baby moments after birth, the act seems to trigger the release of a particular mix of hormones into the mother's blood that stir deep feelings of love for the child. If for some reason the mother is separated from her child immediately after birth, however, the biogrammar is not activated. In this case, bonding takes longer and is harder to establish.

According to Henry, biogrammars control our facial expressions, our instinctive fears and aversions, and our patterns of grammar and syntax. Even by Henry's deterministic measure, however, emotional behavior is not strictly a one-way street of chemicals and prewired response patterns. Just as hormones influence what we feel, our perceptions regularly influence our hormones.

A study of medical corpsmen flying dangerous helicopter missions in Vietnam provides a prime example of this principle at work. In 1970 American researcher Peter Bourne carefully monitored the levels of stress hormones in the blood of these corpsmen on both flying days and off-duty days. Remarkably, he detected no difference. Stranger still, he found the corpsmen's hormonal stress levels to be below those of ordinary people under no particular threat. Similarly low levels of stress hormones were also detected in astronauts and in Vietnam-era Special Forces troops.

Investigators put these findings down to the phenomenon of mind over matter. Significantly, the members of all three of the groups believed that their missions were not dangerous. They felt confident and in control. Moreover, they enjoyed a tremendous esprit de corps as well as a sense that what they were doing was socially valuable. They showed no tendencies toward introspection or morbid fantasizing; they simply attended to the task at hand. Their minds discounted the risk, and their bodies responded accordingly.

Such studies suggest that beyond biological structures and chemical interactions, human emotionality remains fundamentally elusive. Although much has been learned, including the essential role that chemicals play, hardly any scientist would suggest that the complex wash of hormones and neurotransmitters will ever fully paint the portrait of human feeling, even when all the chemicals have been discovered and their mysteries plumbed.

As those studying human emotional development and its evolutionary traces have found, emotional experiences in childhood often occur independently of judgment and memory —the product, perhaps, of ancient neuroendocrine programs that were taking shape before the first mammal ever appeared on earth. As people grow, however, their emotions become inextricably enmeshed in thoughts and values, as well as in the vast network of symbols and words they have devised to define their realities. For every emotion properly codified, a legion defies comprehension. Biogrammars, for example, cannot explain a new mother's willingness to batter or abandon a newborn child. Our fingers do not reveal everything we feel in a sentogram. Emotions mysteriously persist even when their presumed physical circuits are severed. It may well be that some aspect of human emotion will always slip through the scientists' net—a part as individual, ineffable, and inexplicable, finally, as the phenomenon of life itself.

TRACING EMOTION'S PATHWAYS

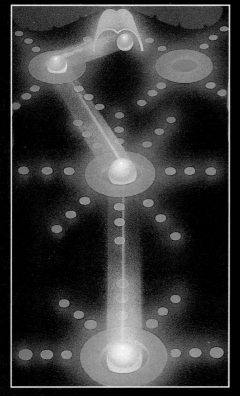

As scientists pursue a more complete understanding of feelings, they are beginning to untangle an intricate puzzle of mind, brain, and body. Though still hard-pressed to put a precise definition to the phenomenon of emotion, most psychologists are sure that feelings involve both conscious and unconscious experiences in the mind, intermingled with a host of reactions in the body. Indeed, emotions seem to be, on a biological level, a rapid-fire sequence of actions and reactions occurring throughout the brain and body—blazing a path that in many ways resembles the wild route

taken by a steel ball as it careers among the bumpers, gates, and tunnels of a pinball machine.

An emotion's unconscious roots begin in the brain's primitive regions. There, a feeling can start to take shape even before any sensation of it penetrates the conscious mind—perhaps explaining why emotions are not always entirely rational. But within an instant, impulses bounce to the cortex—home of memory, awareness, and the higher thinking centers of the brain. At this point, the business of creating and interpreting emotions grows more complex.

The body's reactions to these mental goings-on are equally elaborate. Every emotion generates a characteristic set of physical responses, from the pounding heartbeat of terror to the dizzy euphoria of new love. In many cases, feelings also touch off such specialized—though poorly understood—reflexes as laughing, crying, and blushing. So consistent are these responses that researchers have sometimes been able to figure out what people are feeling simply by monitoring their heart rate and other vital signs. But even as scientists uncover the biological pinball action that goes with feeling a feeling, the physiological components of emotion often remain inseparable from their psychological ones—keeping emotion's fundamental nature shrouded in mystery.

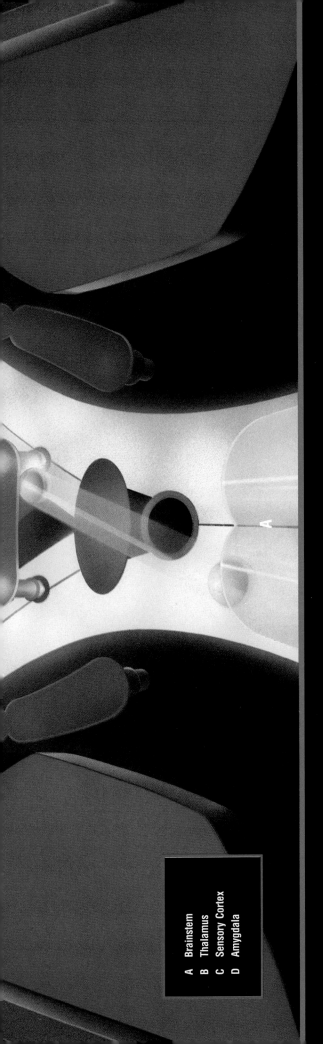

A	Brainstem
B	Thalamus
C	Sensory Cortex
D	Amygdala

EMOTIONS ON THE BRINK OF CONSCIOUSNESS

His thoughts elsewhere, a man absent-mindedly steps off the curb to cross a street—and wanders straight into the path of an oncoming car. In urgent warning, the driver blasts his horn, and within a split second the pedestrian's brain marshals an immediate startled response: His eyes blink, he inhales sharply, and his body stiffens in a jump, even before he can consciously identify the jarring noise or recognize his own sense of alarm.

Traced in the pinball's path above, the process begins when sensory information gathered from the body—here, the ears—enters the brain through one of its most primitive structures, the brainstem (A). Certain centers in the brainstem that respond especially quickly to emotional events shoot preliminary messages to the brain's higher thought centers in the cortex through four major pathways (*arrows*). Each pathway can stimulate the entire cortex, but each favors different areas. One type of stimulus, for example, will cause the

brainstem to send signals to a region devoted to understanding overall patterns, while another will arouse the brain's more analytic powers. In this way, an emotional stimulus can unconsciously influence thought.

As the brainstem alerts other expanses of the brain about information to come, it also bounces specific sensory information—the horn's blast, in this case—to the thalamus (B). The thalamus channels this data to the sensory cortex (C) for conscious assessment and at the same time delivers a jolt to the amygdala (D). Neurologists believe the amygdala endows events with their emotional coloring and significance. The amygdala may use this jump-start from the thalamus simply to prepare for an onslaught of more-sophisticated information, which will soon come from the cortex. However, some experts believe the amygdala can also trigger a basic emotional response—such as the flash of fear caused by the blaring horn—even before the sound's source is understood.

A   Sensory Cortex
B   Frontal Lobe
C   Temporal Lobe
D   Amygdala
E   Hippocampus
    and Septum
F   Hypothalamus
G   Pituitary Gland

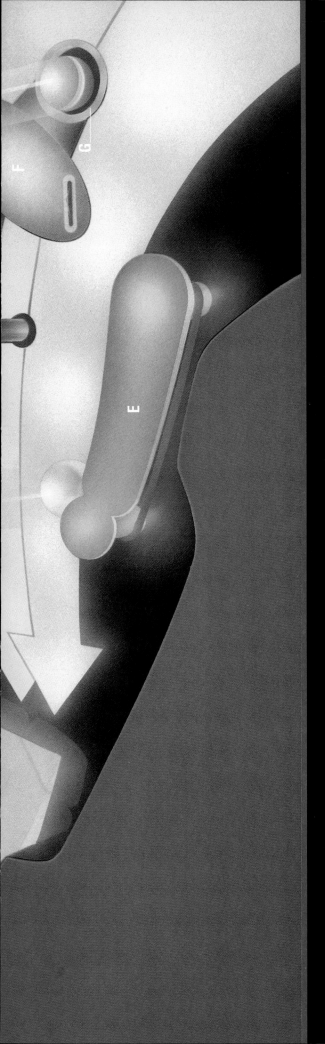

INTEGRATING THOUGHT AND FEELING

Events and emotions rise to consciousness through the convoluted workings of the cortex, even as the rest of the brain continues to process information. As the pinball of emotion speeds along its path, messages travel into the sensory cortex (A), where physical sensations—the blare of a horn, the sight of a rapidly approaching car—are consciously registered. Now, various parts of the cortex join in to help orchestrate an emotional response.

Activity in the left side of the brain seems to create what are commonly thought of as positive emotions, such as amusement or happiness, while the right hemisphere may play a special role in so-called negative emotions—fear, sadness, or anger. However, scientists believe that the right side may be generally more involved than the left in perceiving and expressing any emotion, whether pleasant or not. In addition, individual lobes within each hemisphere carry out distinct functions. The frontal lobes (B) help coordinate thought with motivation and emotional behavior, and both temporal lobes (C) are especially involved in relating memory and emotions—particularly anxiety and

fear, feelings the man in danger on the street is almost certainly beginning to experience.

After information ricochets through the cortex, it bounces back down to the amygdala (D) for further emotional processing. The amygdala also communicates with the hippocampus and the septum (E), two structures that, though connected, play very different roles. The hippocampus may bring up recollections of similar emotional experiences, especially if they are associated with punishment or reward; and the septum, when stimulated, can create feelings described as pure bliss. Indeed, at one point the septum was hailed as one of the brain's key pleasure centers.

The amygdala integrates the complex input from all these parts of the brain and imbues the conscious experience with its emotional tone, completing the entire sequence only fractions of a second after an event is sensed. Then the amygdala passes the ball to the hypothalamus (F) and the pituitary gland (G), which mobilize the body's responses—the trembling hands or racing heart—that accompany these experiences of the mind.

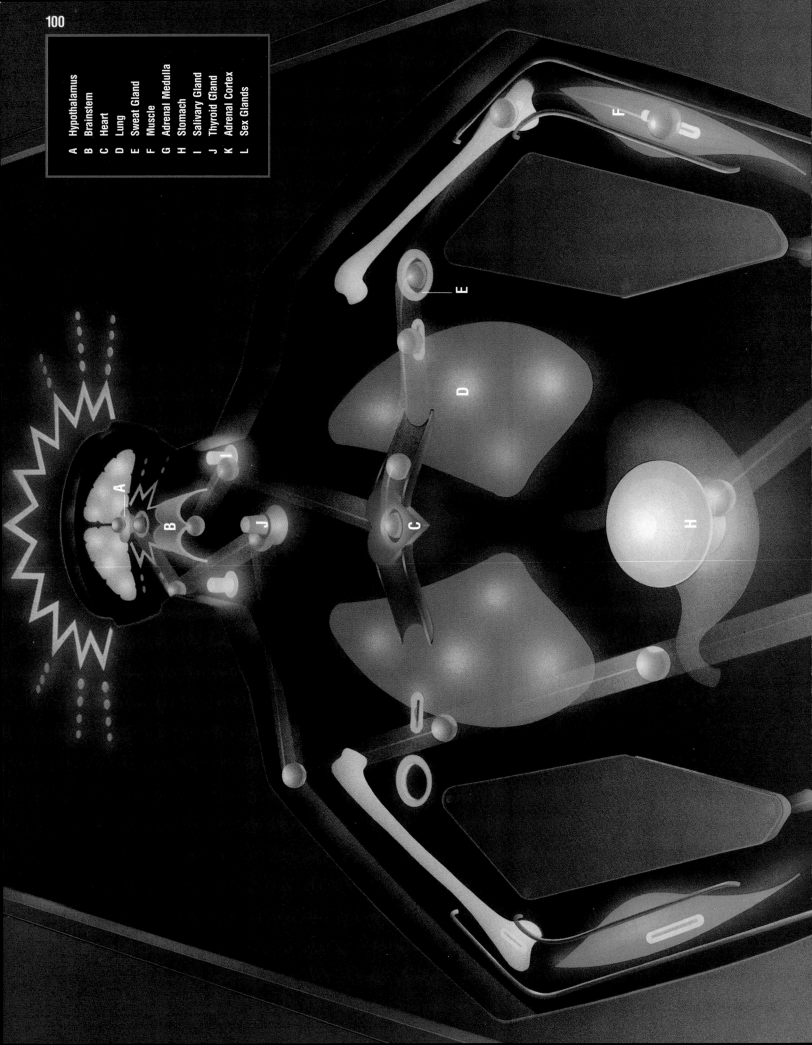

A Hypothalamus
B Brainstem
C Heart
D Lung
E Sweat Gland
F Muscle
G Adrenal Medulla
H Stomach
I Salivary Gland
J Thyroid Gland
K Adrenal Cortex
L Sex Glands

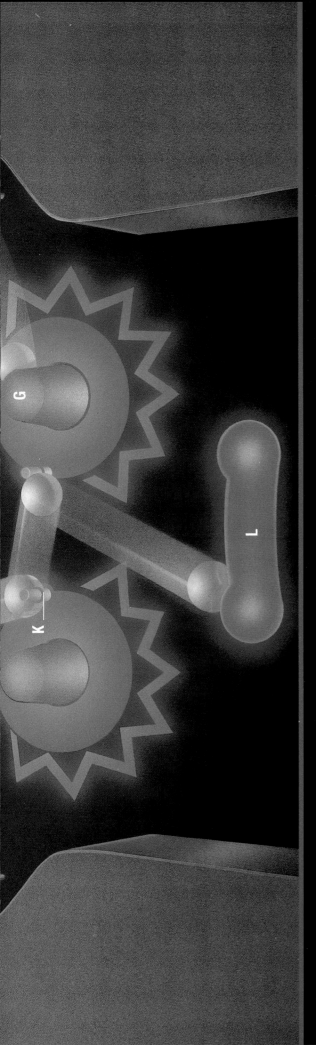

FROM THE BRAIN
TO THE BODY

Once the first impulses that form an emotion have bounced around the brain, the body joins in the game. Typically, the hypothalamus (A) coordinates messages from other parts of the brain and sets in motion an involuntary physical response. For example, the pedestrian suddenly alerted to an oncoming car may feel his heart begin to race and a cold sweat break out over his body even before he has the presence of mind to get out of the way.

Traveling along the web of nerves known as the autonomic nervous system, electrochemical signals (*yellow pinballs*) dart from the brainstem (B) to organs, muscles, and a few glands. In addition, the endocrine system, a network of glands governed jointly by the hypothalamus and the pituitary gland, propels regulatory chemicals called hormones (*blue pinballs*) into the bloodstream. Some hormones target specific organs, whereas some stimulate other glands to secrete hormones of their own.

Among the autonomic nervous system's targets is the brain itself, which releases endorphins during joy and a host of chemicals that produce the euphoric "walking on air" sensation of being in love. The heart (C) and lungs (D) speed up under the influence of most emotions. Sweat glands (E) also work overtime when one is frightened, furious, or in the throes of infatuation, and the extremities often start shaking as muscles (F) are stimulated. Fear, however, seems to be unique in its ability to stimulate the adrenal medulla (G), a gland whose chemicals prepare the body for fight or flight. At such times, the body also slows down activity in organs whose services will not be immediately needed, such as the stomach (H) and salivary glands (I)—explaining why fear often causes the mouth to go dry.

Most endocrine activity occurs under highly stressful emotions, such as terror and rage. The hypothalamus and the pituitary gland release hormones that step up activity in the thyroid gland (J), which accelerates metabolism. These hormones also target the adrenal cortex (K), which in turn secretes a hormone known as cortisol that, among other things, increases blood pressure. Fear actually inhibits activity in the sex glands (L), but anger seems to have the opposite effect: Studies have linked violent behavior with an increased production of testosterone, secreted by sex glands in both men and women.

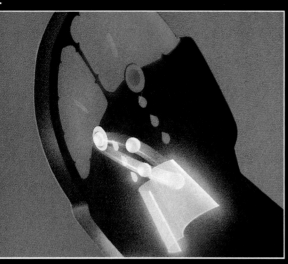

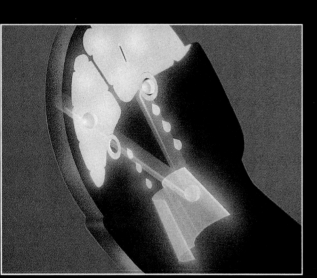

LAUGHING

Researchers have yet to determine why people laugh—and why so many different emotions can evoke the giggles, a mirthful chuckle, or hearty belly laughter. Amusement is certainly the most common trigger, but anxiety, surprise, embarrassment, and even fear are also known to set off the response. Despite their unanswered questions, though, scientists have discovered a great deal about laughter's physical effects—and have turned up some important health benefits along the way.

As the brainstem signals the body to laugh (*below*), the lungs breathe in a characteristic pattern: a deep exhalation followed by inhalation in small gasps. The lungs, in turn, send a message to the heart to beat faster. In many ways this is similar to what happens during exercise, which may be why strong laughter often leaves people with the physically spent though somewhat exhila-rated feeling of just having been through a workout. Furthermore, laughter also stops the stress-related release of cortisol, which can weaken the immune system and cause ulcers and high blood pressure if too much accumulates in the body.

Also intriguing is the possible connection between laughing and crying. It is not without reason that people say they "laughed until they cried," because laughter apparently operates along the same neural routes that produce emotional tears. Scientists spec-ulate that the link may be found in the similar breathing patterns necessary for the two activities.

CRYING

Feelings as diverse as joy, sorrow, and frustration can make a per-son cry. But whatever the cause, all emotional tears spring from the same neural well (*above, left*). When the brain's higher centers decide that tears are an appropriate response, they signal the brainstem, which in turn activates tear glands above and behind each eye. This mechanism differs from the one that generates irritant tears (*above, right*), which rinse the eyes of dust, dirt, and chemicals. When nerves in and around the eye itself sense an irritant, they tell the brainstem to signal the tear glands.

Because two different neural pathways are used, it is possible to sustain brain damage that impairs the tearing ability of one eye but not the other. Still a mystery, however, is why people shed emotional tears at all. The most promising theory is that tears cleanse the body of potentially harmful chemicals that build up during stressful situations. This may explain, at least in part, why people feel better after a good cry.

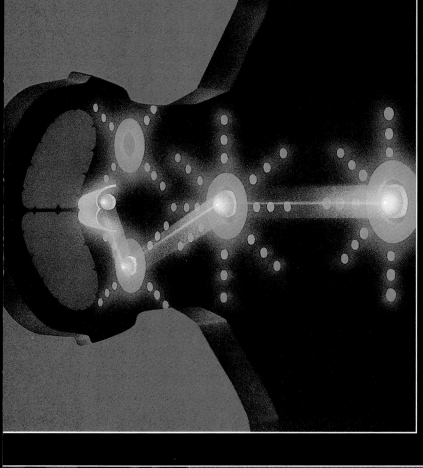

BLUSHING

As with laughing and crying, a variety of emotions cause the uniquely human response of blushing. Biologically, the process is a simple one: The brainstem instructs small blood vessels in the face, neck, and upper chest to dilate (*above*), and as more blood flows into these expanded vessels, the skin takes on a reddish cast. Far less clear, however, is why people blush. Most explanations focus on blushing as a means of communication. When someone does something offensive, for instance, or says something a bit too personal, a blush lets the offender know that he or she has breached the bounds of propriety. Such theories, though promising, fail to explain one remarkable finding: People sometimes blush even when they are alone.

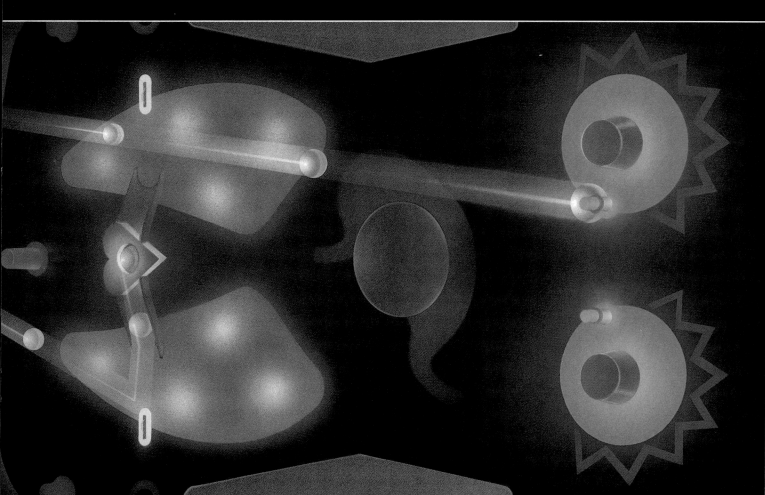

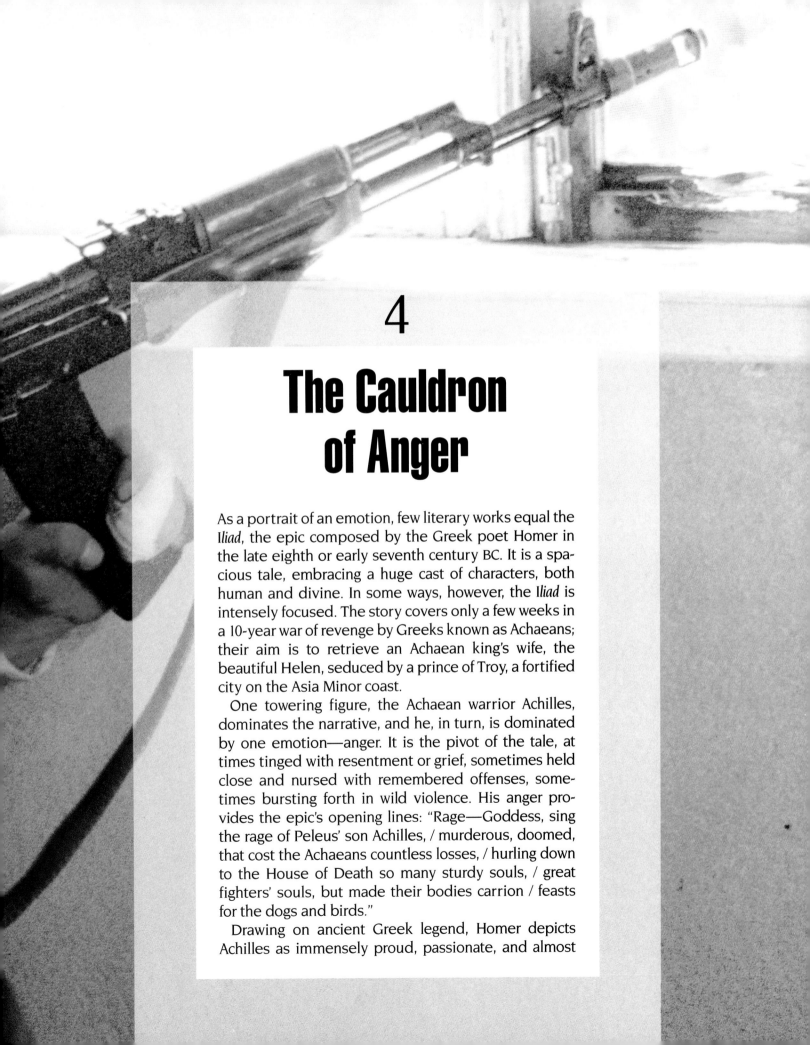

4

The Cauldron of Anger

As a portrait of an emotion, few literary works equal the *Iliad*, the epic composed by the Greek poet Homer in the late eighth or early seventh century BC. It is a spacious tale, embracing a huge cast of characters, both human and divine. In some ways, however, the *Iliad* is intensely focused. The story covers only a few weeks in a 10-year war of revenge by Greeks known as Achaeans; their aim is to retrieve an Achaean king's wife, the beautiful Helen, seduced by a prince of Troy, a fortified city on the Asia Minor coast.

One towering figure, the Achaean warrior Achilles, dominates the narrative, and he, in turn, is dominated by one emotion—anger. It is the pivot of the tale, at times tinged with resentment or grief, sometimes held close and nursed with remembered offenses, sometimes bursting forth in wild violence. His anger provides the epic's opening lines: "Rage—Goddess, sing the rage of Peleus' son Achilles, / murderous, doomed, that cost the Achaeans countless losses, / hurling down to the House of Death so many sturdy souls, / great fighters' souls, but made their bodies carrion / feasts for the dogs and birds."

Drawing on ancient Greek legend, Homer depicts Achilles as immensely proud, passionate, and almost godlike in his fighting prowess. Indeed, divine blood flows in his veins: Achilles' mother, Thetis, is a goddess, and she and other deities advise and assist Achilles—and also restrain his wrath at times. The warrior's rage flows from his deadly quarrel with the leader of all the Achaean forces, Agamemnon. Their confrontation springs from Agamemnon's demand that Achilles give him his concubine, a lovely girl captured in the course of fighting and regarded by Achilles as among his rightful spoils. Enraged, Achilles wonders if he should "draw the long sharp sword slung at his hip, / thrust through the ranks and kill Agamemnon now?— / or check his rage and beat his fury down?"

The goddess Athena, making herself known only to Achilles, urges that Agamemnon be spared. Achilles obeys her and slashes at Agamemnon with words alone: "Staggering drunk, with your dog's eyes, your fawn's heart!" But verbal insults are not enough to assuage his deep sense of injustice. To the dismay of all the Achaean leaders, Achilles swears that he and his men are withdrawing from the war; they will stay by their ships on the shore rather than help the despised Agamemnon.

It is catastrophic news, for the Greeks know they cannot win without Achilles. And, from that moment forward, the war goes badly for the invaders. When a desperate Agamemnon sends his captains to Achilles with placating gifts, they find him as aggrieved and contemptuous as ever: "His gifts, I loathe his gifts."

Only after Agamemnon is wounded and the Achaeans are threatened with annihilation does Achilles relent. He remains unwilling to return to the war himself, but he allows his dearest friend, Patroclus, to fight in his stead and even lends him his armor. In the ensuing battle, Patroclus is killed by Hector, Troy's greatest warrior and crown prince—an event that marks the turning point of the *Iliad*. Distraught, Achilles finally puts his hatred of Agamemnon aside. New armor is made for him by the god Hephaestus. Achilles' anger has also been transformed in the crucible of loss: "A sound of grinding came from the fighter's teeth, / his eyes blazed forth in searing points of fire, / unbearable grief came surging through his heart / and now, bursting with rage against the men of Troy, / he donned Hephaestus' gifts."

Bent on avenging his friend, Achilles slaughters one Trojan after another—a bloodletting that Homer describes in harrowing detail. The defenders make way before the enraged, apparently invulnerable warrior until the combat narrows to the fight between Achilles and Hector—a match Hector knows he is fated to lose but finally accepts. Achilles drives a spear through the brave Trojan. Then, in reply to the dying man's request that his body be returned to his parents, Achilles reveals the full depths of his ferocity: "Would to god my rage, my fury would drive me now / to hack your flesh away and eat you raw." He contents himself with dragging the corpse back to the Achaean camp as though it were some lowly beast rather than a valiant foe.

Achilles' vengeful rampage has turned the tide of war, and now the tale draws to a close. Other literary works would recount what happened next—more mayhem, the death of Achilles, the destruction of Troy. But none of this is described in the *Iliad*. Fittingly, Homer's great epic concludes with a denouement of emotions rather than deeds. At the end, pitying Hector's father, the mighty Achaean warrior permits funereal honors for his fallen enemy. Unstoppable Achilles, the very incarnation of wrath, is quiescent at last, a spent volcano surrounded by the horrific proof of its power.

Homer understood anger as few artists ever have, yet no work of the imagination can do full justice to this protean emotion. Anger comes in al-

Venting Passions on the Airwaves

Since the 1980s, an entrepreneurial twist on the concept of catharsis—the releasing of pent-up emotions—has filled the air with radio and television talk shows. Guided by a celebrity host, visitors speak candidly of their anger, and everything else: abuse, addiction, desertion, deviation—nothing is too personal to disclose. According to the hosts, such exposure brings guests a much-needed emotional relief by allowing them to share their ordeals with the rapt studio audience and the millions listening at home. But there can be a price: Some producers have had to provide counseling for "postshow" trauma.

Although they are quintessentially American, talk shows have become globally ubiquitous. Even in China, where the government has traditionally rationed freedom of expression, these emotional vents are catching on. Radio talk shows now routinely include calls from angry citizens complaining about everything from garbage in the streets to the chilling effects on sexual response of the 1960s Cultural Revolution.

No one fully understands why people tune in to the shows. Perhaps, as the ancient Greek philosopher Aristotle noted in a commentary on the theater, watching others play out a tragedy lets the spectators release their own feelings of anger, pity, and terror.

most infinite variety. Its degrees of intensity can range from simmering annoyance to unbounded, flailing fury. It may be directed at almost anything—at other people, at an unwelcome event or a balky machine, at the world in a general way—or at the self.

As though lurking at the center of the mind's affective apparatus, it is ready to leap into being in reaction to a quarrel, to any perceived slight, betrayal, or threat, to being hurried or delayed, thwarted or exploited, tricked or patronized. Like some highly reactive chemical element, anger may attach itself to anything emotional—to fear, sorrow, bitterness, jealousy, surprise, embarrassment, loathing. It even adjoins love. Indeed, scientists have shown that, although people tend to think of anger as akin to hatred, the usual provoker of anger is a loved one.

The frequency of angry feelings is yet another measure of this emotion's powerful diversity. Studies indicate that most people feel "mild" or "moderate" anger several times a week, and many people report having such feelings several times a day. The pervasiveness of stronger variants of anger is evident in the all-too-rich history of war, crime, and other forms of social and individual discord. Whether buried deep or seething at the surface of consciousness, it is an emotional prime player in human affairs.

The variable nature of anger and its interconnections with other emotions have made this complex of feelings difficult for scientists to define. In the second half of the 19th century, the evolutionist Charles Darwin described emotions as gestures—highly instinctive expressions originating in the distant evolutionary past—that survive in us as vestiges of actions. Anger provided one clear case in point. The baring of teeth in rage, he said, is a gestural remnant of the act of biting. Not long after Darwin offered this evolutionary view of anger, the American philosopher William James proposed a somewhat different explanation. In line with his belief that emotions are simply the brain's interpretations of the body's involuntary reactions to "exciting" situations, he considered anger to be the creature of such bodily sensations, translated into emotion by the mind.

The first scientific study of anger was undertaken in 1894 by American psychologist G. Stanley Hall, who solicited responses from 2,184 men and women to an exhaustive essay questionnaire. Though unsystematic and imprecise, Hall's queries yielded a wealth of fascinating insights into the tangle of sensory and cognitive effects that anger encompasses. The psychologist was astounded by the broad range of physical reactions his respondents reported: scowling, nosebleeds, dizziness, grinding of teeth, clenched fists, goose bumps, numbness, choking, hotness, coldness, blanching, flushing, uncontrolled muscular movements, tears, loss of voice—and on and on. Even more extraordinary were people's often contradictory accounts of how anger made them feel. "I am often frightened that I can get so angry, and often have a nervous headache later," wrote one respondent. Remarked another, "I have found it a not altogether unpleasant sensation to be in a great rage. It wakes me up and makes me feel very much alive."

Indeed, although anger may bring with it a profound feeling of discomfort, it can also be attended by an almost delicious sense of action and release. Achilles, at one point, speaks of anger as "sweeter than dripping streams of honey," and when he finally wades into battle and hews the Trojans left and right, he is the embodiment of martial joy.

Anger's tonic effect was not lost on the great German theologian Martin Luther, author of the Protestant Reformation and a vituperative critic of the abuses that plagued the medieval Catholic Church. "When I am angry," he wrote, "I can write, pray, and preach well, for then my whole temperament is quickened, my understanding sharpened, and all mundane vexations and temptations gone." More than any other emotion, anger appears to foster a sense of prowess that, in many individuals, leads to heightened self-assurance.

This exhilarating quality has led some psychologists to assert that anger is a natural antidote to fear. Christabel Bielenberg, the English wife of a prominent German lawyer during World War II, experienced this proposition firsthand. In 1945 Bielenberg was summoned to a bleak office on Berlin's Prinz Alberechstrasse to respond to accusations that she had plotted to kill Adolf Hitler. Her husband had already been interned in Ravensbrück prison on suspicion of the same charge.

"Oh, I was terrified when I got there—I was so weak at the knees I could hardly get up the steps," Bielenberg recalled later. As she awaited her arraignment in the vestibule, however, she witnessed a scene that radically altered her feelings. A Nazi official, incensed that a prisoner had asked to read his "confession" before signing it, struck the man across the face. Aghast at the brutality, Bielenberg felt a flame of white-hot rage envelop her. "I was so angry it just wasn't possible to go on being frightened," she recalled. The fury served her well. Over the course of her nine-hour interrogation, Bielenberg's unwavering composure and flinty resolve convinced the Gestapo that she was innocent. They let her go, and subsequently freed her husband as well.

So closely linked are anger and fear, in fact, that researchers have often found it difficult to tell them apart on a physiological level. A few decades ago, for example, psychophysiologist Albert Ax carried out an experiment to discover if anger could be physiologically distinguished from fear. Volunteers were wired to a polygraph that measured heart rate, blood pressure, muscle tension, and sweating; they were then subjected to frightening stimuli or to anger-producing insults and other abuse. The differences in the polygraph responses were not great, but Ax thought he saw distinct hormonal influences at work.

The polygraph readings brought on by fear were similar to physiological reactions known to be induced by an injection of epinephrine, or adrenaline. The association between fear and epinephrine was well documented, but Ax was convinced that anger's polygraph pattern could be ascribed to a combined upsurge of epinephrine and norepinephrine (noradrena-line), another hormone produced by the adrenal gland. Further studies, however, put the lie to this tidy equation. Both epinephrine and norepinephrine, it turns out, are involved in both emotions, with fear linked to higher levels of epinephrine, anger linked to higher levels of norepinephrine. And because anger shades into so many other emotions, its physiological character is also tinged by the hormones and neurotransmitters associated with other feelings.

Whatever anger's chemical relationship to fear may be, psychologists of Freudian persuasion tend to see anger as invariably linked to aggression. The aggression may be turned outward, producing such feelings as rage or detestation, or it may be blocked and turned inward, producing depression, guilt, or shame.

Other psychologists dispute such linking. "People often experience anger without taking any aggressive action," observes Albert Bandura of Stanford University. "Conversely they can be induced to perform injurious acts without accompanying anger." As to the primary causes of anger, Freud's heirs give considerable weight to supposedly unresolved problems of childhood, whereas many other psychologists focus on the world immediately at hand. Bandura, for example, has proposed four stimuli that are most likely to provoke an angry re-sponse: verbal insults or threats, physical assaults, the thwarting of an activity, or the deprivation of some reward. Certainly, in his embodiment of anger, the warrior Achilles was responding to all four.

In 1981 American psychologist Janet Polivy set out to clear the air with a definitive profile of anger, describing both its physiological and its psychological aspects. She conducted a series of experiments in which volunteers were deliberately placed in anger-provoking situations and then interviewed about their feelings. The results surprised her: No profile emerged from the responses. Instead, Polivy's subjects reported feeling not only anger but also a smorgasbord of other emotions, including anxiety, depression, hostility, and sadness. Anger seemed to be a central figure in a complex emotional web, all of whose strands were subtly interconnected and none very well understood.

The effect of culture appears to make that web still more difficult to read. In her 1989 work *Anger: The Misunderstood Emotion*, social psychologist Carol Tavris observes that "people everywhere get angry, but they get angry in the service of their culture's rules." Those rules—attitudes and values that can be difficult for an out-sider to detect—vary enormously around the world.

One of the extremes in that varia-tion are the !Kung people of the Kala-hari Desert in southern Africa. Before they were assimilated into modern settlements, the !Kung subsisted al-most entirely on wild vegetables and game, which they gathered from the area around their campgrounds. They moved their camps every few days or weeks as they foraged for new sources of protein. This nomadic mode of life required members of each band, which usually numbered about 35, to cooperate closely and suppress per-sonal differences. Although the !Kung experienced the same disappoint-ments and irritations as other people, they had learned to blunt the expres-sion of feelings so as not to wrinkle the social fabric. One anthropologist who spent almost a year and a half among these people saw only four in-stances of overt discord. Indeed, ag-gression played so minimal a part in their way of life that the !Kung were dubbed "the harmless people" by American author-naturalist Elizabeth Marshall Thomas.

Anthropologists visiting a !Kung camp observed that children were kept under close supervision by adults. When the inevitable squabble broke out, elders quickly stepped in to separate the troublemakers and

Fears and Phobias: Anger's Other Side

Although anger is clearly one of the most potent and destructive of human emotions, fear—which some psychologists have identified as the other side of the coin of rage—has great power all its own. To some people, for example, a photograph from the top of California's Golden Gate Bridge (*left*) is enough in itself to produce the vertigo that comes from a fear of heights. Such irrational but paralyzing apprehensions are called phobias, from the Greek word for panic or fear.

People can be morbidly afraid of anything: animals or children, heat or cold, dark or light, open spaces or closed ones, even themselves. Some people, in fact, have a fear of everything, a condition known as panophobia. Confronted with a dreaded object or situation—usually made frightening by some forgotten prior experience—a phobic person is overwhelmed by the physical and mental symptoms of anxiety, even to the point of paralysis.

Phobias are difficult, but not impossible, to cure. Behavioral techniques such as systematic desensitization, where a phobic person is taught to relax in the presence of a variety of fearsome stimuli, have been effective. Sometimes organizations take a hand: Airlines now refer people to programs that help them overcome one of the modern world's common terrors—the fear of flying.

restore peace. A child who threw a tantrum was unlikely to find it rewarding: !Kung adults simply ignored the squalls. By the time children reached adolescence, they had learned to channel their angry feelings into harmless gestures. As an example, one anthropologist told of a case in which a young woman insulted her father and was then rebuked by him and by other members of the group; she was clearly incensed at the way she had been chastised, but her response was to put a blanket over her head and sit sulking under cover the entire day. This kind of sulk was standard among the !Kung: The person judged to be in the wrong withdrew and turned frustrations inward.

Cultural discouragement of displays of anger is by no means confined to peoples living a marginal existence. Tavris points to Japanese restraint as an example. "An individual who feels very angry is likely to show it by excessive politeness and a neutral expression instead of by furious words and signs," she writes. "A Japanese who shows anger the Western way is admitting that he has lost control, and therefore lost face." By contrast, in other cultures, notes Tavris, "a man may lose face if he does *not* show anger when it is appropriate and 'manly' for him to do so."

The degree to which any kind of sentiment is expressed varies greatly around the world. In many Arab cultures, the tendency is toward extremes of enthusiasm or distaste. As

T. E. Lawrence—the British adventurer known as Lawrence of Arabia—put it, there are "no half-tones in their register of vision." The polarity is perhaps clearest in attitudes toward anger and sadness. While Arabs tend to admire self-control, they also accept extreme outbursts of both these emotions. In much of the Arab world, it is not considered a fault suddenly to give way to a fit of temper. People commonly use angry shouts and gestures in the process of bargaining for goods in the marketplace. There is a pervasive tolerance of drama and emotion, reflected in the Syro-Lebanese proverb "At each meal a quarrel; with each bite a worry."

Italy has also produced a highly demonstrative people. Journalist Luigi Barzini, author of a witty national portrait titled *The Italians*, described his fellow citizens' animation this way: "Conversations can be followed at a distance by merely watching the changing expressions of those taking part in them. You can read joy, sorrow, hope, anger, relief, boredom, despair, love, and disappointment as easily as large-printed words on a wall poster. Undisguised emotions, some sincere and some feigned, follow each other on an Italian's face as swiftly as the shadows of clouds over a meadow on a windy day in spring."

For any given emotion, the Italians can draw on a large gestural repertoire, especially in displaying shades of anger. As scholarly evidence, Barzini cites a 19th-century Neapolitan priest's list of the many ways in which anger may be silently expressed—among them, "biting one's lips, biting one's hands and single fingers, tearing one's hair, scratching one's face, firmly enclosing one fist in the other hand and rubbing it with such force that the joints crack, gnashing one's teeth with wide open lips, moving one's lips with a shuddering, nervous rhythm, stamping the ground with violence, beating palm against palm, as if to applaud, once or twice only, with force." Not surprisingly, angry deeds sometimes

accompany angry words and gestures. "Italy," says Barzini, "is a bloodstained country" with numerous killings over love, honor, prestige, money, politics, and all the other elements that inevitably funnel into rage.

The bloodshed is nothing recent. Ancient Rome was a famously turbulent place, astir with aggressive energies that helped build a great empire but also threatened the social and political framework of that empire on countless occasions during its long history. In the first century AD, the philosopher Seneca—an adviser to the emperor Nero and an adherent of the Roman philosophical school known as Stoicism—wrote a lengthy treatise titled *On Anger*. He viewed the emotion as profoundly destructive: "Behold the most glorious cities

Both anger and aggressive competitiveness—feelings common to athletes in such rough-and-tumble sports as rugby *(left)*—have been shown to raise levels of testosterone in men, and the hormone has been linked to violent male behavior. But cultural conditioning, some scientists believe, can be as important as chemistry in determining how, or even if, powerful emotions will be expressed.

whose foundations can scarcely be traced—anger cast them down. Behold solitudes stretching lonely for many miles without a single dweller—anger laid them waste."

The only sensible way of dealing with this most dangerous of emotions, Seneca said, was to keep it under rigorous control, to chain it up as though it were a lion or a tiger. According to Seneca, people should make every effort to avoid becoming angry, and if their efforts at self-control did not suffice, they should be sure to hold the outward expression of their anger to an absolute minimum. The philosopher went so far as to counsel that a person aspire only to goals that were clearly within reach; in his judgment, failure, frustration, and their aftermath of anger were simply too great a threat to order.

Philosophical arguments for anger control were an old story by Seneca's day. Four centuries earlier, the Greek philosopher Aristotle had taught that holding anger in check was a sign of mental strength: Only weak people gave vent to fury. To kick at inanimate objects or rail about trivial matters was akin to being drunk or insane. On the other hand, Aristotle believed, there was nothing inherently evil

about anger, and its expression could at times be appropriate.

During the Middle Ages, when Christianity dominated Europe, the philosopher Thomas Aquinas championed such a view within the church. He called anger a "desire to punish another by way of just revenge." For example, deliberate injury was fair cause for retaliation, in Aquinas's view. He went further, arguing that it was a vice not to show wrath in some cases, because acquiescence to wrongdoing encouraged other misdeeds.

All of these strands of thought helped to shape Western standards of behavior, as did the teachings of the Bible. Scripture held a complex message, however. The God of the Old Testament could be angry on the grandest imaginable scale, punishing misdeeds and faithlessness with floods that covered the earth, destruction of cities, calamitous military defeats, pestilence, famine, and more. In the New Testament, Jesus of Nazareth prescribed an ethic of mercy, love, and turning the other cheek. But this gentle new spiritual leader was not beyond anger, as he demonstrated in his spirited hurling of the moneychangers from the temple steps.

Given the varied threads of the West's intellectual heritage, it is not surprising that, as late as the 17th century, European cultures had still evolved no simple code of conduct for

angry behavior—certainly none so well defined as the codes that kept anger under tight control in many Asian societies. But the attitudes of Europeans, both at home and in America, were changing.

In their 1986 book, *Anger: The Struggle for Emotional Control in America's History*, psychiatrist Carol Stearns and her husband, historian Peter Stearns, have traced how anger became socially codified. Examining letters, diaries, sermons, novels, and articles in the popular press of the day, they have identified distinct phases in the evolving "forms, perceptions, and possibly, levels of anger" in America.

Displays of strong emotion were a familiar feature of life in 17th-century America, the authors note. Husbands and wives fought openly; parents reacted to the disobedience of children with anger designed to break their will; public insults were heard everywhere and resulted in innumerable trials for slander; quarrels were common at all levels of society; and outsiders—such as foreigners or people of a different religion—were subjected to particular vitriol. None of this contentiousness excited much comment, much less worry. As the authors put it: "Anger was too normal, too anticipated to be seen as a problem."

By the 18th century, a desire to control anger had emerged. It seemed traceable to several factors. The intellectual movement known as the Enlightenment held that humans should keep their anger in check because they are, above all else, reasoning creatures. The Enlightenment also advanced the view that humans—including outsiders—are, in principle, equal and should therefore be regarded with tolerance. Increasing literacy helped foster the ideal of rationality. At the same time, the population was growing rapidly, and economic relationships were becoming more complex—developments attended by an increasing need for rules of civility.

Vocabulary reflected the shift in attitudes. At the end of the 18th century, the word *tantrum* made its debut. Perhaps derived from the term *tarantella*—a kind of frenzied dance—it referred to outbursts of anger by adults and was decidedly negative in its connotations. (It would not acquire its current association with small children until much later.) Around the same time, the word *temper* began to take on a pejorative hue.

The 1830s and 1840s witnesses escalating social disapproval of anger, especially in the home, which was described as a "sacred enclosure"—a refuge from a tumultuous world undergoing industrialization. Popular literature brimmed with cautionary tales about marriages ruined by a single quarrel. Angry individuals were portrayed in fiction as people of bad character, and magazines were filled with advice about avoiding domestic discord: "Cultivate a spirit of mutual and generous forbearance, carefully avoiding anything like angry contention or contradiction." This injunction applied to men as well as to women. One book of advice for husbands declared, "Quarrels of every sort are exceedingly destructive of human happiness; but no quarrels, save those among brethren in the church, are so bitter as family quarrels."

Still, men and women were seen as different in the matter of anger. Although men were not supposed to express the emotion, they were expected to feel it. In one short story, for example, a woman says of her husband, "Tom was spirited and quick-tempered—great, loving-hearted men always are." In women, however, anger was supposed to be perfectly absent, not even felt. According to the social canons of the day, note the Stearnses, "anger and femininity were antithetical." As for children, they might exhibit irritation at times, but the example of their parents would inevitably serve to counteract these deplorable tendencies and to produce good behavior in the end.

The unattainability of perfect harmony at home may actually have produced an increase in anger in 19th-century American marriages, according to the Stearnses. In any case, the code shifted subtly during the latter half of the 19th century and the first few decades of the 20th. For one thing, it was a time of frenetic entrepreneurial activity, in which some forms of aggression became functional in the context of two-fisted capitalism. For another, society had a new awareness of evolutionary links between humans and animals, behavioral as well as physical. The Enlightenment view of the authentic human self as rational had to be modified: Instincts, including combative ones, had to be accepted as part of the basic human makeup.

Thus, a parent should expect to see fighting spirit in a boy—although it should not be given free rein, of course. Child-rearing manuals recommended that boyhood anger be channeled into sports and other character-building forms of competition, and giving a boy a pair of boxing gloves became a widespread middle-class custom. With girls, however, the channeling of anger was deemed unnecessary. In the popular view, there was nothing to channel.

Further adjustments in America's stance toward anger followed as the 20th century advanced. Advice givers in the popular press began to acknowledge that disagreements were a normal part of marriage. Children were allowed, and even encouraged, to express angry feelings at home, the theory being that anger could safely drain away there. Indeed, there was a growing sense that, if not handled properly, anger could fester and cause greater trouble later in life. But the overall cultural rules still amounted to a policy of anger containment. Marriage counselors told troubled couples that an inability to patch up quarrels was a sign of "immaturity." Corporations, worried that open anger in the workplace would reduce the effectiveness and productivity of their employees, trained supervisors in anger-defusing skills. Today, the Stearnses conclude, America still adheres to views of anger that took shape in the 18th century—a strategy of restraint, of keeping the lid on.

Some researchers think that current economic trends favor even more containment. One of those trends is a slackening of growth in manufacturing and an expansion in service industries—airlines, fast-food restaurants, financial-service companies, and the like. In many service businesses, pleasing the customer is critical, and angry confrontations are to be avoided at all costs.

In the 1980s, sociologist Arlie Russell Hochschild decided to examine how service companies approach this delicate issue. During the course of her investigations, she attended classes for flight attendants at a major airline. Hochschild discovered that the attendants were required to undergo "Recurrent Training" every year. One of its goals was to help workers, most of them women, learn to cope with obstreperous passengers without themselves getting angry.

Appealing to the attendant's sense of professionalism, the course instructor described the task in a special jargon, referring to rude customers as "irates." Flight attendants were taught to "handle" the irates just as they would a class of grumpy children. The instructor described how she quelled her own hostile feelings toward angry passengers: "I pretend something traumatic has happened in their lives," such as the death of a relative. This refocusing would shift her attention away from her own feelings and onto the customer's wishes—a

"The best methods of governing an impetuous temper are various. I will suggest a few which appear to me most worthy of attention.

"Consider, in the first place, what there is in life which is worth getting into a passion for. It is foolish 'to level dread artillery at a fly.'

"Consider, in the next place, what you will be likely to gain by anger. The more you indulge it, the more you may. Give an inch, in matters of this sort, and an ell will be demanded. It is much easier to subdue your temper when you have been angry but once, than when you have been angry twice."

process termed "anger desensitization" in the sessions. The effect of such training, in Hochschild's judgment, was to put emotional blinders on the employee. She argues that, in time, it could cause them to lose touch with their "true selves."

Most service companies are far less systematic in addressing the issue of anger in customers and employees than the airline Hochschild studied. But her general concern—what she called "the commercialization of human feeling"—cannot be lightly dismissed. By her calculation, about one-third of the people employed in the United States have jobs that require "emotional labor" to some degree. They must suppress their own hostility, following a path of meek tranquillity through a noisy crowd of hectoring customers. This, of course, takes an emotional toll of its own, not the least of which is chronic worry about displaying one's pent-up rage.

Such concerns are pervasive in modern society. Many people, from all walks of life, worry about their anger —about its effects on their career or their home life, about its frequency and unpredictability, about their inability to control it as society suggests they should. Some people seek help, often as a stopgap measure to promote calm during moments of stress, but sometimes as a long-term program of therapy to get at what Freudians would consider the deeper causes of the problem, such as childhood trauma. The remedial options for both the immediate and the enduring disturbances of anger are numerous, although there is little agreement among subjects or experts about the efficacy of these techniques.

Vigorous physical activity is one of the traditional remedies for excess anger. For many years it has been widely believed that exercise could drain off or deflect the emotional energy that might otherwise erupt destructively as anger, although there is little scientific evidence for this. In the early 1970s, for example, psychologist Dolf Zillmann, then a professor at the University of Pennsylvania, paid student volunteers to participate in a sham learning experiment during which some of them received mild shocks, administered to provoke an angry response. The number and intensity of the shocks varied, with some participants getting more or stronger jolts than others. Next, the volunteers were required to do various amounts of exercise. Finally, they administered shocks to other subjects and could choose the intensity of the shocks—which would presumably reflect the intensity of their anger.

Zillmann, with colleagues Aaron Katcher and Barry Milavsky, reported that the volunteers who had been most provoked by shocks at the beginning of the experiment were also likely to administer stronger shocks themselves—regardless of the amount of exercise that they had done. In another experiment, Zillmann and two co-workers, Rolland Johnson and Kenneth Day, found that subjects who were more physically fit were likely to administer less-severe shocks. The reason for this, the researchers concluded, might be that people who are fit relax more rapidly after a state of excitation—or provocation—and thus experience less aggression.

But in 1975 a doctor at the Harvard Medical School turned the activity-relieves-stress idea on its head. Too much activity, not too little—particularly when that activity is frenzied—is the bane of American society, argued heart specialist Herbert Benson. Searching for ways to treat what he viewed as general hyperactivity, Benson arrived at a technique that he called the relaxation response and wrote about it in a book that became a runaway bestseller.

Benson believed that not enough attention is given to environmental stress as a source of heart attacks and strokes. He argued that the many small battles modern humans fight

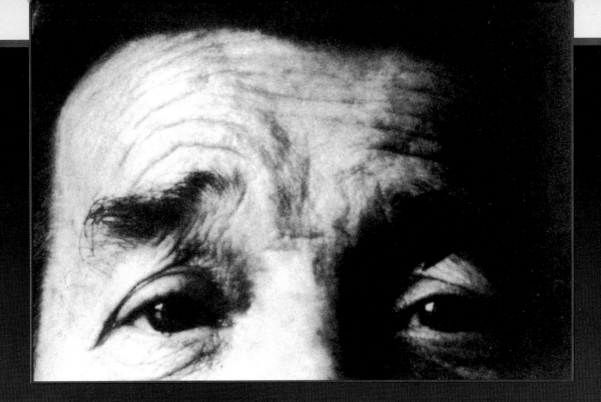

Facing Depression

One out of every 20 Americans will suffer a major depression during his or her lifetime, and yet the symptoms of what is clinically known as unipolar disorder often go unrecognized, mistaken for something else or even dismissed as "the way things are." Typical signs of clinical depression last at least two weeks and include a mood of hopelessness and a loss of interest in things that were once pleasing, such as family life, hobbies, and career. Sleep disturbances, inexplicable fatigue, changes in appetite, an inability to concentrate, and recurring thoughts of death or suicide can also torment the sufferer.

One subtle sign, visible for others to see, is a facial expression known as Veraguth's fold (*above*). A triangle-shaped fold in the inner corner of the upper eyelid, the feature was first noted by Swiss neuropsychiatrist Otto Veraguth during studies demonstrating that certain muscles of the face undergo changes in tone during both mild and major depression, and during depressive phases of the mood disorder commonly known as manic depression but usually referred to by physicians as manic-depressive, or bipolar, disorder.

The term *bipolar* refers to the extreme ends—or poles—of the spectrum of human emotion. Manic depression is known to be a disease in which periods of "normal" feelings and functioning are punctuated with phases of intense highs and lows. During high, manic episodes, people with the disorder may have an unrealistically elevated sense of their abilities or importance, and they may be persistently excited or irritable. Much more energetic than usual, they may need little sleep and be extraordinarily productive, their minds may race from thought to thought, and they may talk to excess—for example, spending several hours at a stretch on the telephone. Unrestrained shopping sprees, sexual misadventures, and impulsive business deals are also not uncommon for manic episodes.

Unipolar and bipolar disorders have been recognized since at least 400 BC, when Hippocrates coined the terms *mania* and *melancholia* to describe periods of great exhilaration and despair, and scientists now agree that the two are different aspects of the same disease. According to 19th-century German psychiatrist Emil Kraepelin, who formulated the clinical description of manic depression that is still in use, the symptoms of the depressive episodes in the disorder are identical to those experienced unrelentingly during unipolar depression.

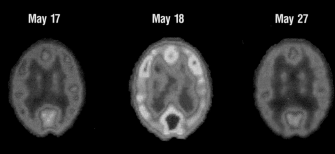

May 17   May 18   May 27

CHARTING MANIC DEPRESSION. Three PET scans—taken of the same patient on May 17, May 18, and May 27, 1983—illustrate a physiological change that occurs in the brain during different phases of bipolar disorder. The predominant shades of blue in the first scan, performed when the patient was depressed, indicate that glucose was being metabolized at a very low rate. By the following day, however, the patient had become mildly manic—or "hypomanic"—and the brain image taken then signaled a much higher metabolic rate in the red and yellow areas. The third scan reveals that the patient reverted to a state of depression nine days later.

Manic Depression and the Artistic Temperament

More rare than simple depression, bipolar mood disorder afflicts one person for every five suffering the unipolar variety. Researchers are certain, however, that both forms have biological roots resulting from a combination of genetics and environment. The prominent role of genetics has been borne out by numerous family studies, including several showing that when one identical twin has a bipolar disorder, the other twin's chance of experiencing it is at least 70 percent.

One expert on manic depression in artists and writers supports a retrospective diagnosis of the disorder in Vincent van Gogh, for example, with biographical histories of the painter's family. Of his four siblings, three displayed evidence of serious mental illness—and one of them committed suicide. Van Gogh himself was tormented by devastating mood swings and displayed the extraordinary productivity of mania: During his stay in Auvers-sur-Oise, France—shortly before his own suicide in 1890—he painted 70 pictures in as many days, two of which are shown at right.

Many scientific investigations have verified the notion that artists, writers, poets, composers, and musicians suffer from a significantly higher rate of mood disorders than the general population. A particularly illustrative study conducted during the 1980s at the University of Iowa Writers' Workshop found that 80 percent of the study participants met the formal diagnostic criteria for a major mood disorder. Indeed, the connection between madness and creativity extends beyond sheer numbers of anecdotal tales of artistic temperament. Both the creative and the manic mind share thought patterns that are fluid, rapid, and flexible—and they share the ability to splice and fuse this flood of ideas into innovative expressions as well. The difference lies in whether the artist controls the thoughts or vice versa.

The chemistry of mood disorders has been traced in part to a dysfunction of either the neurotransmitters norepinephrine, serotonin, and dopamine or of the nerve synapses involved with their transmission. Medications are now available for the treatment of mood disorders—and they are most successful when used together with some method of psychotherapy. Although some artists fear they will lose their creative edge if their extreme mood swings are brought under control, the suicide rate of those who suffer from mood disorders is as high as 20 percent—making diagnosis and treatment as critical for unipolar and bipolar depression as for any other potentially lethal disease.

House at Auvers, Vincent van Gogh, June 1890

Field with Poppies, Vincent van Gogh, June 1890

during the day are more wearing than those experienced by our ancestors, whose simpler lives were mostly spent foraging. Nowadays we have to dodge bad drivers on the freeway, adjust to frequent job moves, cope with persistent cultural change, and battle unruly children. These crises, according to Benson, evoke the physiological fight-or-flight response—in which the body pumps epinephrine through the system to increase alertness. One side effect of increased alertness is an elevation in average blood pressure, which causes the arteries to deteriorate and the heart to weaken. Among other sources of support for this view of the deleterious effects of modernity, Benson cited data from Puerto Rico showing that many people who moved from the quiet countryside into cities experienced an increase in blood pressure.

As a way of tapping into the relaxation response—the calm counterpart of the fight-or-flight response—Benson offered a form of meditation without religious trappings. He studied Zen monks, Himalayan mystics, and particularly the followers of the Maharishi Mahesh Yogi. Members of the maharishi's group in the United States—adherents of the transcendental meditation movement—visited Benson's laboratory at Harvard and participated in a series of experiments. Later, Benson extracted what

he regards as the four key elements of their relaxation technique and taught these elements as part of a program that could take the stress—and the anger—out of people's lives.

To be effective in bringing forth the relaxation response, Benson said, a technique must include the repetition of a word, sound, prayer, or phrase, and passive disregard of everyday thoughts for at least 20 minutes. As proof of the technique's benefits, Benson cited a study of 86 volunteers that showed a decline in blood pressure from borderline highs to average values after several weeks. But the same study also noted that the reduced blood pressure lasted only for the relatively brief period of time that the relaxation response itself was in effect; when it stopped, blood pressure rose to its former levels.

Physical activity and meditation are only two options among many that have been explored in the search for ways to control anger. Music has long been an alternative of choice. The Greek philosopher Plato wrote, "Rhythm and harmony find their way into the secret places of the soul, bearing grace in their movements, and making the soul graceful." Most research has focused on the possible

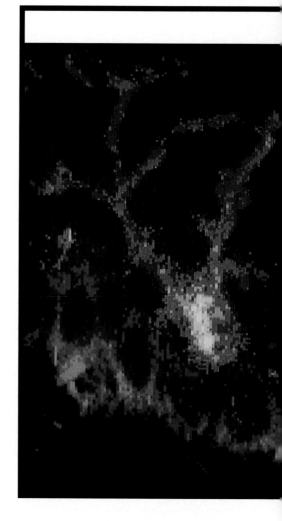

use of music as a way of relaxing the tensions that cluster around angry feelings. In one study, university students who listened to "soft and relaxing" music exhibited a measurable decline in anxiety in a written test designed for this purpose; the music proved just as soothing as both physical and meditative routines specifi-

Feelings That
May Be Only Skin Deep

When the mind is stressed by anger or other strong emotions, the body often seems to reply with disorders of the skin. Now it appears that the key to that still-unverified linkage may be the immune system's Langerhans' cells (*orange, at left*) in the skin's top layer (*green*). Their day-to-day function is to monitor the skin's surface through hair-like tendrils, and to attack intruders, thus triggering a secondary offensive by white blood cells. But the response of Langerhans' cells appears to vary.

Work by Richard Granstein of Massachusetts General Hospital and George Murphy, a pathologist at the University of Pennsylvania, shows that Langerhans' cells connect to nerve cells in the skin's top layer—nerve cells that can secrete the chemical CGRP, which suppresses the Langerhans' cells' immune function. According to Murphy and Granstein, the amount of CGRP may be changed to modulate Langerhans' cell activity. Hypothetically, at least, stressful emotions could alter the release of CGRP, influencing the function of Langerhans' cells. Thus, through a still-unknown mechanism, changes in CGRP release could set the stage for outbreaks of such skin disorders as psoriasis—and, perhaps, for seemingly spontaneous healing.

cally designed to relax the muscles. A follow-up study showed a rise in skin temperatures among volunteers who listened to calming music—another sign of muscle relaxation.

Music, meditation, and exercise can clearly help defuse anger in specific circumstances, but most psychologists would agree that any serious problems in coping with anger require a broader approach. Even so, at least in the opinion of one therapist, treatment may involve no more than some simple changes in lifestyle. Psychologist Michael Argyle believes that ordinary activities offer a therapeutic key. He points out that people who are chronically depressed or angry often find themselves stuck in a rut, oppressed by the feeling that there is no escape. He and some colleagues have devised a way to boost patients out of such a state, essentially by teaching them how to have a good time: eat a good meal, read a good book, enjoy the scenery, spend more time with friends. They ask patients to keep a diary, logging the number of times each month they have an enjoyable experience. With encouragement, and with their diary as a kind of baseline, people learn to increase the frequency of pleasant activities and thereby increase their overall happiness.

Some people grappling with the presumed deep-seated roots of anger choose therapies that owe their view of emotion to Sigmund Freud. Like so many pioneers, he drew upon the technology of his day to describe the way anger operates. The psyche was like a steam engine, he said, in which anger boils into a gas, condenses back into some manageable emotion, and boils up again.

The resulting school of thought proposed a way of managing anger that Freud might actually have despised. When the pressure inside the metaphorical boiler becomes too great, argued these so-called ventilationists, you simply let it out. This notion has inspired huge diversities of treatments, from ripping at towels and punching pillows to uttering what are called primal screams—techniques intended to vent anger and believed at the time to reduce its force. Recent psychological studies have found, however, that letting off steam only lets off steam and does little to resolve underlying difficulties. Indeed, it may reinforce, rather than dilute, angry feelings. As Carol Tavris points

Back to the Womb's Muffled Symphonies

The belief that music can calm even such tempestuous emotions as rage is universal among humans. Indeed, music is now known to mitigate the anxiety and pain of illness and to dampen destructive feelings. But the Tomatis method goes further. Named for its discoverer, French physician Alfred Tomatis, the therapeutic technique purports to take its subjects back to the womb, at least acoustically.

A human fetus begins to hear at just 18 weeks, both with its newly developed ears and with its resonating body. Muffled by amniotic fluid and the mother's bulk, sounds reaching the fetus are in the higher-frequency range above 8,000 hertz (cycles per second)—comparable to the pitch of flutes. What the fetus hears in this range teaches it to listen, which, Tomatis believes, is the key to the way the person eventually adapts to the external world. If, for some reason, that learning process is disturbed, subsequent adaptations may be affected as well.

In the Tomatis method, adults listen for hours to a specially concocted medley that may include such things as a mother's voice and a Mozart concerto, with sounds below 8,000 hertz filtered out. This supposedly restores the listener to the acoustic conditions of the womb, where the interrupted learning processes can resume without interference. Administered by some 200 centers worldwide, the technique has been credited with successfully treating such dysfunctions as depression, anxiety, panic, and sexual-abuse trauma.

out, the discovery that ventilationism "just doesn't work" is one of the major accomplishments of anger studies.

A number of psychologists, dissatisfied with the ventilationist strategy, have devised a kind of learning approach to emotional troubles, a method known as cognitive behavior therapy. In contrast to Freudian tactics of probing the unconscious mind for festering, coded frustrations, cognitive therapy targets conscious ideas that affect emotion. "Psychological problems are not necessarily the product of mysterious, impenetrable forces," says one of its pioneers, psychiatrist Aaron Beck. Instead, they may result from simple errors, such as behavioral distortions that originate in poor learning during a child's development, a misreading of events, or a failure to distinguish clearly between what is real and what is imagined.

With regard to why we feel anger, Beck concludes that the common incitements can be narrowed to just a handful. People get angry if they think they have been directly attacked by someone else, especially if the attack seems intentional. They lash out against violations of law or social mores. And they can become aroused if they sense that their personal domain has been violated.

The last category includes a broad area of potential trouble. For example, people who believe they are en-

titled to a great deal of attention may become angry when someone else steals the show at a party; they see the hubbub around the other person as a personal loss. This, says Beck, is an example of faulty thinking. The task of the cognitive therapist is to help someone with such erroneous ideas to understand how and why the ideas are wrong. If a person's thoughts are seriously off track, the cognitive therapist must try to help the person retrace his or her mental steps and find a better path.

Several variations of cognitive behavior therapy have emerged over the years. Perhaps the most distinctive is rational-emotive behavior therapy, invented by psychologist Albert Ellis in the 1950s. It has elements in common with the Roman philosophy of Stoicism; indeed, Ellis says he hit upon it while he was reading the great philosophers and at the same time trying to cure himself of his chronic shyness. The essence of the technique, he states, is to promote "scientific" thinking and to teach ways of avoiding self-defeating behavior.

To make it easier for people to examine their thought processes, Ellis devised a simple therapeutic drill acronymically named ABC. The A

stands for the activating event that supposedly caused the disturbance—being turned down for a job, for example. B is for the belief used to interpret the event—thinking the rejection means that one is worthless, for instance. And C is for the consequences or neurotic symptoms produced by the event—depression, perhaps. Ellis's scheme teaches people to dissect and criticize their own belief systems. Its motto is taken from the Stoic philosopher Epictetus: "People are disturbed not by things, but by the views which they take of them."

A common cause of anger, Ellis observes, is a threat to one's self-esteem. His therapy aims to teach people not to build their feelings of self-worth upon other people's opinions; to do so creates a "fragile" sense of well-being. Ellis also notes that many troubled people exhibit what he calls "low frustration-tolerance anger." That is, they believe that "the world has to be arranged so that I get pretty much what I want, when I want it, without too much hassle." This is an unrealistic idea, he says: Dispense with it and minimize anger.

Another variant of cognitive behavior therapy is a multistep process known as stress inoculation, designed by Donald Meichenbaum of the University of Waterloo in Ontario, Canada, to help people cope with such stress producers as phobias and speech anxiety. The technique was later broadened to cover the stresses of rape, combat, medical anxiety, and the like.

The stress inoculation process has three parts. Phase one is educational and calls for the therapist to elicit general information about the problem and propose a course of treatment. At this stage, Meichenbaum says, it is important that patients view the process as "plausible" and become collaborators. Second comes the rehearsal phase, during which patients are taught specific coping techniques: deep breathing and muscle relaxation to combat the physical responses to anxiety; and cognitive exercises to overcome self-defeating thoughts. As part of this drill, patients may repeat phrases such as "One step at a time—you can handle the situation." Then comes the final, application phase—the inoculation itself. Patients are asked to try out the new skills in real stress-inducing situations, but the stress is delivered in graded doses so that the patients gain confidence in their coping skills.

Psychologist Raymond Novaco of the University of California has applied this method to so-called problem anger. One of Novaco's early experiments involved clients who recognized that they were having serious trouble controlling their anger—people who, when enraged, physically assaulted others and destroyed property. Following the Meichenbaum prescription, he gave the volunteers a three-step inoculation: They were made aware of their thoughts and feelings when provoked, were taught cognitive relaxation and behavioral skills, and then were helped to practice those skills while imagining and playing roles in anger-producing situations. Measurements of their physiological arousal and multiple measures of anger indicated "a striking improvement in the ability to regulate and manage anger," according to Novaco. The key to Novaco's technique: It transforms what had once seemed like a threat demanding retaliation into a problem requiring a solution.

Although cognitive therapies seem to work well on individuals willing to examine their inner thoughts, these techniques do little for less amenable people whose bad tempers land them in trouble. It was to help such hard cases that Arnold Goldstein of Syracuse University created another type of therapy called structured learning. Working with a group of six to 12 people at a time, the therapist acts as a teacher and drama coach. Problem topics—such as an inability to express a complaint in a constructive fashion—are analyzed in detail.

The trainer breaks the required skills into four or more well-defined steps. For example, the recommended steps for expressing a complaint are these: 1) define what the problem is and who is responsible; 2) decide how the problem might be solved; 3) tell the responsible person what the problem is and how it might be solved; 4) ask for a response; 5) show that you understand his or her feelings; 6) come to an agreement on the steps to be taken by each of you.

The group tries to learn these steps one by one, as trainers act out constructive patterns of behavior. All the members of the group take turns playing roles, discuss one another's performances, and practice their "scripts" at home. Although the newly learned skills may not work when used for the first time in real life, Goldstein claims that trainers are successful about 50 percent of the time in teaching people how to cope with difficult events.

In the last decade, a different and distinctly Asian technique for coping with emotions has gained popularity in the United States. Called Morita therapy after its founder, Masatake Morita, chairman of the psychiatry department at the Jikei University

An Open and Shut Case:
Two Very Different Therapies

The cultural variations in the ways people express anger and anguish may be seen most clearly in the types of therapies designed to treat them. At one extreme, the Western reflex toward openness has spawned primal therapy, in which people are encouraged to regress to early memories of parental neglect, and then release emotions by acting them out.

Formulated by California psychologist Arthur Janov in the late 1960s, primal therapy requires both locating and reexperiencing one's wrath at early trauma: Janov investigated the remedial effects of such actions after one of his patients howled in fury at his own parents during a therapy session. Early accounts of primal therapy included reports of participants who sobbed, sucked their thumbs, and whimpered as they relived infant frustrations. Janov claimed that, with their tensions eased, the patients could resume life as neurosis-free adults.

At the other extreme is Japan's Morita therapy, in which the Freudian view that neuroses arise from past traumas is replaced by a concept of character development. In formulating his technique, psychiatrist Masatake Morita relied heavily on the Zen Buddhist principle of the acceptance of pain and suffering as a normal part of life. In effect, Morita patients are trained to live with their neuroses. They progress through four stages of successively more disciplined behavior, from an initial period of bed-bound isolation, to one of light work, then to one of hard manual labor, and finally to a stage in which life can again be shared with others. After completing a successful course of Morita therapy, individuals are supposedly able to carry out everyday activities despite the continued presence of previously disabling emotions.

Medical School, this method of self-discipline arose in Japan around the turn of the 20th century and made it across the Pacific in the late 1970s. The exercise has found a receptive audience among business people and others interested in what its proponents term "character development." Grounded in Zen Buddhism, it emphasizes an acceptance of emotions, including fear and anxiety. Morita therapists tell their clients (properly called "students") that they should not attempt to wipe away such feelings but should recognize that they are natural, and concentrate on changing behavior. Confrontation is seen as a source of dissatisfaction rather than relief; instead, Morita therapy asks students to reflect on how to fit more harmoniously into their situation.

Morita originally created his therapy to treat a particular form of neurosis in which sufferers become withdrawn, oversensitive, and hypochondriac. But U.S. followers have adapted it to other purposes. For example, Gregg Krech, a certified instructor in a Morita-derived therapy called Constructive Living, applies similar techniques to resolving conflicts in the workplace. In Constructive Living workshops, he tries to show people how to avoid becoming fixated on feelings of resent-ment. An aggrieved person, according to this instruction, should neither vent anger immediately nor keep it buried. Instead, Krech tells students to sit on a grievance for a few days, think about it carefully, and if the matter still seems important, speak calmly to the other party. The advice makes sense in principle but may be easier to apply in a workshop than in the real world, where the steam of anger often shatters the fragile vessels in which we try to contain it.

Curiously, the prospect of anger loosed into the world is for many peo-ple less a source of anxiety than the age-old dilemma of expressing this powerful emotion in socially and morally acceptable ways. Social com-mentators Carol and Peter Stearns have described the United States as a country that is especially and chron-ically uneasy on this score. "We worry that if we express ourselves we will ir-ritate our spouses to the point that they will desert us or we will reveal ourselves as immature," they write. "We accept that it is legitimate, even necessary, to express some anger, but then we torture ourselves about whether we are doing it in the right way, at the right time, perhaps too lit-tle, perhaps too much. We strive for consistency. We seek to manage our tempers and adhere to the same goals in our relationships at home as in those at work. We raise our children to act the same way. But we are not comfortable with ourselves."

Comfort, however, would seem to be the one thing that anger is not about. It can be suppressed, diverted, or deemed inappropriate by the ration-al mind, but to some degree, it must always remain untamable—incorri-gibly independent. Although Achilles' unchecked rage, "sweeter than drip-ping streams of honey," may hold lit-tle appeal, who would want to lose the ability to experience feelings of such magnitude? We would like, per-haps, to be free of the anger that sinks us in fear, but we would regret the loss of the anger that brings us to courage. A silly business when seen in tantrums, anger glows with purpose when mobilized in a just cause.

Ultimately, anger is not merely use-ful but seems to be central, a kind of jewel in the emotional crown. A spec-trum of emotions without anger would be like a palette without the color red; it would be life without emotion —not really life at all.

THE TANGLED WEB OF DECEPTION

Although deception occurs in nature, it appears that only human beings lie. Indeed, to an adult futilely trying to find the truth in an adolescent alibi, lying may seem maddeningly pervasive. It is certainly true that the world does not love a liar: Falsehood corrodes every social contract, whether the lie is that of a misbehaving child or of a corrupt politician.

Its calculatedness makes the act of lying seem to spring from guile, but lying is often impelled by emotion—fear or anger, sadness or love. The physical expression of these emotions may also expose the liar. As early as 900 BC, a Hindu medical expert wrote that liars blush and run their fingers through their hair. To University of California psychologist Paul Ekman, such behavioral signals are the preferred way to tell if someone is lying. More than two decades' study has taught Ekman that liars salt their speech, expressions, and body language with telling signs.

To lie successfully, Ekman posits, a liar must overcome three major hurdles: the fear of getting caught, the shame of telling a lie, and the joy of getting away with it, or, in Ekman's shorthand: detection apprehension, deception guilt, and duping delight. Such feelings are modulated by the liar's personality, the magnitude and kind of lie, and who is being lied to. To the astute observer, hints of these emotions can expose all but the most skilled deceivers—those who can lie without leaving an emotional trace.

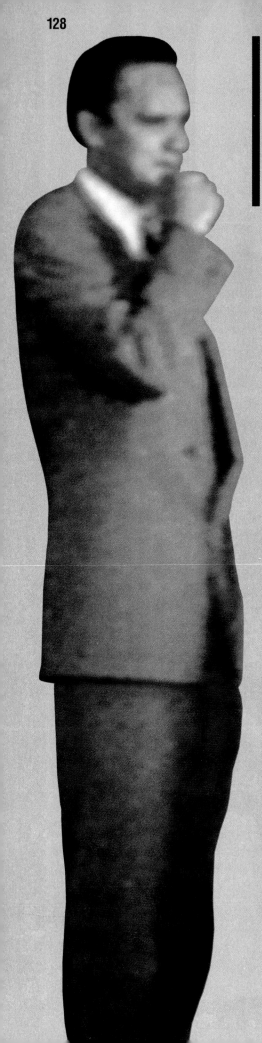

MANIPULATOR. Finding a detective in his office, a nervous Tim Robbins exhibits a manipulator: He scratches his chin, communicating nervousness but not necessarily deception. As his interview with the police unfolds, the usually smooth movie executive exhibits more and more manipulators, a possible sign of his detection apprehension.

LOSING HIS COOL. Peppered with questions, Robbins blinks, gestures with his hands, and looks away from the detective, signaling his nervousness. Ekman notes that an averted gaze may indicate anxiety, but he warns that such signs require careful evaluation: An accomplished liar has no problem making eye contact.

ANGRY EYES. In spite of his efforts to appear calm under the continuing interrogation, Robbins's eyes and lips reveal his anger. His eyebrows have lowered and drawn together with vertical lines between them, and the tight, flat set of his lips is a universally recognized sign of anger.

THE UNIVERSAL LANGUAGE OF LIES

Liars seldom betray themselves by a single flaw in their falsehood but instead leave a trail of faint clues. Fleeting facial movements called micro-expressions, though rare, are among the most reliable of these. Although they last for only a split second, micro-expressions are complete expressions that can reveal a concealed emotion to trained lie catchers. Also damning is the more common squelched expression, which occurs when a person interrupts an unwanted expression before it fully forms.

Facial muscles, such as those in the forehead, often betray the liar because they are difficult to control. Blinking and sweating, though not direct signs of deception, may indicate nervousness or fear. What Ekman calls emblems include shrugs, head nods, and hand waves; occurring incompletely or out of context, they may signal deception. Movements called manipulators include such actions as hair twisting or scratching, and they increase with nervousness.

In these four still shots of actor Tim Robbins, from the film *The Player*, Robbins's character is a movie executive who denies committing a murder. Viewers know Robbins is lying because they saw him kill a man, but they might sense the falsehood anyway: The actor amplifies the subtle signals of lying in a way that the audience instinctively comprehends. Because such tacit understanding is rare in the real world, however, Ekman and others prescribe extreme caution in trying to diagnose a liar.

DUPING DELIGHT. Convinced that he has fooled the detective, a cocksure Robbins cannot hold back a smile as his interrogator leaves. The actor demonstrates the smug smile of duping delight, reflecting the high spirits that, for some, make lying an irresistible, even addictive, challenge.

Is today Wednesday?

Do you know Mr. Q?

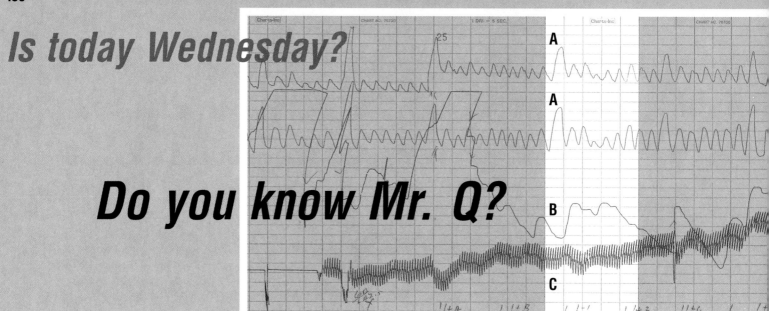

Do you live at 10 Main Street?

THE TRUTH. An honest response to a control question on a polygraph chart *(white band, above)* is marked by the absence of dramatic changes in the two lines for breathing (A), and single traces for hand sweating (B) and blood pressure and pulse (C). A strong deviation in the lines could indicate lying.

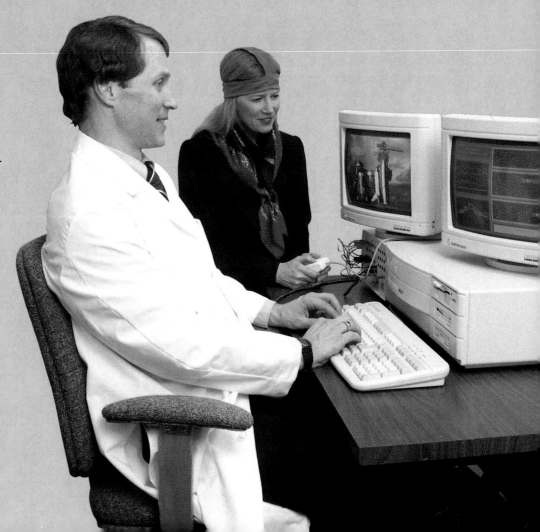

NEW FRONTIERS. Demonstrating his MERA system, neuroscientist Lawrence Farwell flashes video images to a subject, who wears electrodes that measure her brain's electrical activity. The screen shows three kinds of images: crime-related, non-crime-related, and general images shown to all subjects before the test. Brain-activity traces *(far right)* reveal recognition by differences in the shape of a blue line. A green trace shows the response to irrelevant data, and a red line traces the response to images seen preceding the test.

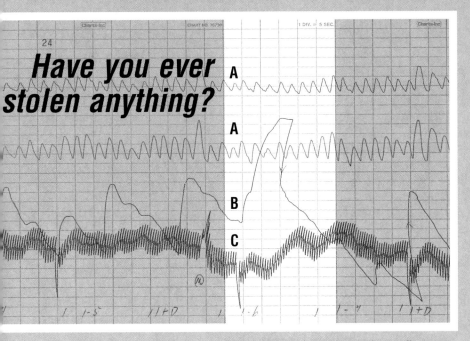

Have you ever stolen anything?

A
A
B
C

Did you steal the $500?

THE LIE. As a subject responds to a direct question about a crime *(white band, above)*, the polygraph lines begin to leap, signaling deceit. A slight but steady rise in the peaks of lines A indicates increasingly deep breaths, and the dramatic increase in line B shows increasing perspiration on the subject's hands. Line C records a skipped heartbeat as a question is asked, followed by a steady rise in blood pressure.

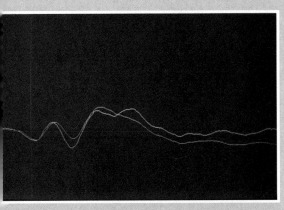

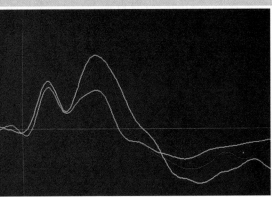

A THIN BLUE LINE. One subject shows only a slight rise in the blue line *(left, top)*, suggesting that the material presented signifies nothing to him. But a second subject exhibits a steep rise followed by a sharp dip in the blue line *(bottom)*, a pattern that shows recognition of the material—in this case, by a store owner who was robbed.

SEISMOGRAMS OF FALSEHOOD

The polygraph offers a mechanical, and controversial, alternative to the subtler business of reading clues in a liar's physical behavior. The device measures pulse, blood pressure, breathing, and sweating—all autonomic nervous system functions—as the subject is questioned, and converts these into electrical signals expressed as lines on a running graph.

Polygraphers employ an array of questions, mixing incriminating, direct ones—"Did you steal the $500?"—with innocuous ones. By comparing the autonomic signals sensed by the instrument, and by watching for clues in the subject's behavior, polygraphers try to expose the guilty. Some polygraphers claim as high as 90 percent reliability, but critics counter that the autonomic functions of an innocent subject may jump during a test simply because the person is nervous or upset, thereby skewing the results.

This problem may have been solved by Lawrence Farwell, a Maryland neuroscientist, who is developing a device that does not rely on autonomic responses. His MERA (multifaceted electroencephalographic response analysis) system tests whether a subject recognizes information related to an event by measuring brain electricity. According to Farwell, recognition produces a distinct electrical pattern. Although the device is not a lie detector, MERA might spot a criminal's denial of being at a scene that he or she secretly recognized.

"...The tougher it gets, the cooler I get."

"I probably did not have a clear recollection of the matter then."

"We have pulled out of all our military bases abroad."

POOR MEMORY. "I probably did not have a clear recollection of the matter then," hedged Japanese prime minister Noboru Takeshita, seen announcing his resignation in April 1989. Takeshita had finally been forced to concede that he and his supporters had knowingly received nearly a million dollars from Japan's influence-seeking Recruit Company.

STRATEGIC FALSEHOOD. "We have pulled out of all our military bases abroad," fibbed Soviet premier Nikita Khrushchev, seen during a 1959 speech to the National Press Club in Washington, D.C. Khrushchev told his lie shortly before his government emplaced medium-range ballistic missiles in Cuba, sparking the 1962 crisis.

WATERGATE. "The tougher it gets, the cooler I get," lies President Richard Nixon as he denies allegations of wrongdoing at a November 1973 press conference. His nervous animation and heavy perspiration tell another story, later confirmed by press disclosures of corruption and cover-up that led to Nixon's resignation on August 9, 1974.

MENDACIOUS MAYOR. "You don't believe all that stuff, do you?" Washington, D.C., mayor Marion Barry asked rhetorically as he went on trial in 1990 for 11 drug charges and three counts of perjury. In fact, many people did. Barry's denials failed against a videotape that showed him smoking crack cocaine, and he was convicted of drug possession.

LIE STYLES OF THE VERY FAMOUS

Among liars, a minority excels at spinning false tales and enjoys doing it. According to Paul Ekman, these deceivers bring two crucial tools to the job: They can plan a lie so that it seems credible, and they have the nerve to carry it off without physiological signals. Their edge is that they feel neither detection apprehension nor deception guilt.

Such skills may be put to work to deceive a spouse, boss, or enemy, or in such careers as espionage and acting. But when natural liars come to power, their deceptions can alter the course of history. In September 1938, Nazi dictator Adolf Hitler was a notorious case in point. During a series of face-to-face meetings in Munich, he told British chancellor Neville Chamberlain that Germany had no designs on Czechoslovakia; Chamberlain went home echoing Hitler's lie and became a symbol of appeasement. The Munich meeting demonstrated another liar's rule of thumb: Success often relies on the victim's wishful thinking.

Adolf Hitler may have made the Big Lie an instrument of national policy, but he was not the only lying leader. The impulse to deceive cuts across culture, race, and time, as seen in this gallery of four famously untruthful contemporary figures.

"You don't believe all that stuff, do you?"

GLOSSARY

Adrenal glands: two small glands, located just above the kidneys, that consist of two parts: the cortex, or outer layer; and the medulla, or inner layer. Various hormones produced here are involved in the physical aspects of an emotional response, such as increased blood pressure during anger.

Adrenaline: *See* Epinephrine.

Amygdala: part of the limbic system that processes sensory input, especially smell, and also helps generate emotions.

Anxiety: mental distress caused by the anticipation of threat or danger; a vaguely fearful feeling.

Autonomic nervous system: the system of nerves that regulates normally involuntary bodily processes, such as blood pressure, heart rate, breathing, and digestion, all of which can fluctuate during an emotional reaction. Part of the peripheral nervous system, the autonomic nervous system consists of sympathetic and parasympathetic divisions. *See also* Parasympathetic nervous system; Sympathetic nervous system.

Brainstem: the part of the brain that is continuous with the top of the spinal cord. The brainstem consists of the medulla, the midbrain, and the pons, and is involved in the routing of all incoming and outgoing nerve signals.

Brain waves: fluctuations in the electrical activity of many brain cells as recorded on an electroencephalogram (EEG). Brain wave frequency indicates an individual's state of consciousness—active, relaxed, asleep, and so on.

Cerebral cortex: the thin outer layer of the cerebrum in mammals. The cortex is responsible for higher brain functions such as learning, thought, and memory.

Cerebral hemispheres: the two divisions of the cerebrum, also known as the left brain and the right brain. The left brain is thought by some to be primarily analytic and verbal in function; the right brain, visual and intuitive.

Cognitive therapy: a form of psychological treatment that focuses on correcting distorted or maladaptive thinking.

Cortex: the outer layer of an organ or structure; the cerebral cortex.

Duchenne Smile: a facial expression, indicative of true happiness, that is characterized by upturned lips and wrinkles around the eyes; named for the neurologist who first mapped the facial muscles' movements.

Electroencephalogram (EEG): a graphic record of the brain's electrical activity, consisting of patterns of fluctuating waves. *See also* Brain waves.

Endocrine system: the body's network of glands and other organs that secrete hormones, which trigger some of the body's physical responses to emotion.

Epinephrine: a stress-related hormone, produced by the adrenal glands, that increases heart rate, blood pressure, and carbohydrate metabolism; also known as adrenaline. Epinephrine is also produced by neurons and functions as a neurotransmitter.

Facial feedback hypothesis: the theory that making a certain facial expression will produce the corresponding emotion.

Fight-or-flight response: the central and sympathetic nervous systems' reaction to threat or stress, which quickly prepares the body for conflict or escape. The response involves the release of epinephrine and is typically triggered by fear.

Hippocampus: part of the limbic system of the brain, involved in the storage and retrieval of memories and in the generation of emotions.

Hormones: chemicals, released by glands and a few other organs, that travel through the bloodstream and regulate the activities of specific tissues, organs, and other glands.

Hypothalamus: a structure in the brain that controls many autonomic functions, such as body temperature regulation, and also produces hormones and neurotransmitters, thus playing an important role in the physical manifestations of emotions.

Limbic system: the collective term for several related structures within the brain that play a major role in emotion, memory, and the regulation of certain autonomic functions.

Magnetic resonance imaging (MRI): a procedure that uses magnetic fields and radio waves to provide a highly detailed map of an interior structure of the body, such as the brain.

Midbrain: the uppermost of the three segments of the brainstem, serving primarily as an intermediary between the rest of the brain and the spinal cord.

Nervous system: the entire system of nerves and nerve centers in the body, including the brain, spinal cord, nerves, and ganglia.

Neurotransmitter: any of a number of chemical substances, synthesized by neurons, that are involved in the transmission of electrochemical impulses across the synaptic gap from one neuron to another or from a neuron to a muscle or gland.

Noradrenaline: *See* Norepinephrine.

Norepinephrine: a hormone, produced by the adrenal medulla, that constricts blood vessels and raises blood pressure; also known as noradrenaline. Norepinephrine is also produced by neurons and functions as a neurotransmitter.

Parasympathetic nervous system: one of two divisions of the autonomic nervous system. The parasympathetic nervous system typically acts in balanced opposition to the sympathetic nervous system, functioning to bring the body back into homeostasis, or internal equilibrium.

Phenylethylamine (PEA): a naturally occurring amphetamine-like substance that plays a role in stimulating romantic love.

Pituitary gland: a structure, located in the brain near the hypothalamus, that controls all other glands in the body through the release of hormones.

Rational-emotive therapy: a technique of cognitive therapy that focuses on rejection of irrational beliefs that lead to mental distress and maladaptive behavior.

Socialization: the process through which an individual learns the attitudes and behavior appropriate to his or her social environment.

Spinal cord: a thick cable of nerves and associated nerve cells, housed within the backbone, that relays impulses between the brain and the rest of the body.

Sympathetic nervous system: one of two divisions of the autonomic nervous system. The sympathetic nervous system stimulates the body and is most active during states of arousal.

Testosterone: a hormone that primarily affects male sexual behavior and is involved in aggression in both sexes.

Thalamus: a structure within the brain that initially processes all sensory input except smell and routes the input to the cerebral cortex.

BIBLIOGRAPHY

BOOKS

Abu-Lughod, Lila. *Veiled Sentiments.* Berkeley, Calif.: University of California Press, 1986.

Alcott, William Alexander. *The Young Husband, or, Duties of Man in the Marriage Relation.* Boston: George W. Light, 1840.

Allen, Larue, and John W. Santrock. *Psychology: The Contexts of Behavior.* Madison, Wis.: Brown and Benchmark, 1993.

Anderson, John R. *Cognitive Psychology and Its Implications* (3d ed.). New York: W. H. Freeman, 1990.

Argyle, Michael. *The Psychology of Happiness.* New York: Routledge, 1987.

Averill, James R.:
Anger and Aggression. New York: Springer-Verlag, 1982.
"The Structural Bases of Emotional Behavior." In *Emotion,* edited by Margaret S. Clark. Newbury Park, Calif.: Sage, 1992.

Barclay, Lisa K. *Infant Development.* New York: Holt, Rinehart, and Winston, 1985.

Barzini, Luigi. *The Italians.* New York: Atheneum, 1965.

Beck, Aaron T. *Cognitive Therapy and the Emotional Disorders.* New York: Meridian, 1976.

Benson, Herbert, with Miriam Z. Klipper. *The Relaxation Response.* New York: Avon Books, 1975.

Birren, Faber:
Color and Human Response. New York: Van Nostrand Reinhold, 1978.

Color Psychology and Color Therapy. New York: Carol Publishing Group, 1992.

Blechman, Elaine A., ed. *Emotions and the Family: For Better or for Worse.* Hillsdale, N.J.: Lawrence Erlbaum Associates, 1990.

Bloom, Floyd E., and Arlyne Lazerson. *Brain, Mind, and Behavior* (2d ed.). New York: W. H. Freeman, 1988.

Buck, Ross. *The Communication of Emotion.* New York: Guilford Press, 1984.

Carlson, John G., and Elaine Hatfield. *Psychology of Emotion.* New York: Harcourt Brace Jovanovich College Publishers, 1992.

Clark, Margaret S., ed.:
Emotion. Newbury Park, Calif.: Sage, 1992.
Emotion and Social Behavior. Newbury Park, Calif.: Sage, 1992.

Clayman, Charles B. (ed.). *Encyclopedia of Medicine.* New York: Random House, 1989.

Clynes, Manfred. *Sentics: The Touch of the Emotions.* Dorset, England: Prism Press, 1989.

Coles, Michael G. H., Emanuel Donchin, and Stephen W. Porges (eds.). *Psychophysiology: Systems, Processes, and Applications.* New York: Guilford Press, 1986.

Crane, Stephen. *The Red Badge of Courage.* New York: Avon Books, 1982.

Critchley, Macdonald, and R. A. Henson. *Music and the Brain.* Springfield, Ill.: Charles C. Thomas, 1977.

Darwin, Charles. *The Expression of the Emotions in Man and Animals.* Chicago: University of Chicago Press, 1965.

Deutsch, Diana (ed.). *The Psychology of Music.* New York: Academic Press, 1982.

Diamond, Jared. *The Third Chimpanzee: The Evolution and Future of the Human Animal.* New York: HarperPerennial, 1993.

Doi, Takeo. *The Anatomy of Dependence.* Translated by John Bester. New York: Kodansha International, 1981.

Draper, Patricia. "The Learning Environment for Aggression and Anti-Social Behavior among the !Kung." In *Learning Non-Aggression,* edited by Ashley Montagu. New York: Oxford University Press, 1978.

Ekman, Paul. *Telling Lies.* New York: W. W. Norton, 1992.

Ekman, Paul, and Wallace V. Friesen. *Unmasking the Face.* Palo Alto, Calif.: Consulting Psychologists Press, 1975.

Ellis, Albert. *How to Live with—and without—Anger.* New York: Reader's Digest Press, 1977.

Ellis, Albert, and Russell M. Grieger. *Handbook of Rational-Emotive Therapy.* New York: Springer, 1986.

Fisher, Helen E. *Anatomy of Love: The Natural History of Monogamy, Adultery, and Divorce.* New York: W. W. Norton, 1992.

Frey, William H., II, with Muriel Langseth. *Crying: The Mystery of Tears.* Minneapolis: Winston Press, 1985.

Fridlund, Alan J. "The Behavioral Ecology

and Sociality of Human Faces." In *Emotion*, edited by Margaret S. Clark. Newbury Park, Calif.: Sage, 1992.

Frijda, Nico H., et al. "The Complexity of Intensity: Issues concerning the Structure of Emotion Intensity." In *Emotion*, edited by Margaret S. Clark. Newbury Park, Calif.: Sage, 1992.

Goldstein, Arnold P., and Leonard Krasner. *Prevention and Control of Aggression*. New York: Pergamon Press, 1983.

Goodenough, Judith, Betty McGuire, and Robert A. Wallace. *Perspectives on Animal Behavior*. New York: John Wiley and Sons, 1993.

Gregory, Richard L. (ed.). *The Oxford Companion to the Mind*. New York: Oxford University Press, 1987.

Guyton, Arthur C. *Textbook of Medical Physiology* (8th ed.). Philadelphia: W. B. Saunders, 1991.

Harris, Paul L.:
Children and Emotion. New York: Basil Blackwell, 1989.
"Understanding Emotion." In *Handbook of Emotions*, edited by Michael Lewis and Jeannette M. Haviland. New York: Guilford Press, 1993.
"What Children Know about the Situations That Provoke Emotion." In *The Socialization of Emotions*, edited by Michael Lewis and Carolyn Saarni. New York: Plenum Press, 1985.

Hatfield, Elaine, John T. Cacioppo, and Richard L. Rapson. "Primitive Emotional Contagion." In *Emotion and Social Behavior*, edited by Margaret S. Clark. Newbury Park, Calif.: Sage, 1992.

Hatfield, Elaine, and Richard L. Rapson. "Emotions: A Trinity." In *Emotions and the Family: For Better or for Worse*, edited by Elaine A. Blechman. Hillsdale, N.J.: Lawrence Erlbaum Associates, 1990.

Henry, J. P., and P. M. Stephens. *Stress, Health, and the Social Environment*. New York: Springer-Verlag, 1983.

Hochschild, Arlie Russell. *The Managed Heart*. Berkeley, Calif.: University of California Press, 1983.

Homer. *The Iliad*. Translated by Robert Fagles. New York: Penguin, 1990.

Hope, Augustine, and Margaret Walch. *The Color Compendium*. New York: Van Nostrand Reinhold, 1990.

Howell, Signe. "Rules Not Words." In *Indigenous Psychologies: The Anthropology of the Self*, edited by Paul Heelas and Andrew Lock. New York: Academic Press, 1981.

Izard, Carroll E. *The Psychology of Emotions*. New York: Plenum Press, 1991.

Jamison, Kay Redfield. *Touched with Fire: Manic-Depressive Illness and the Artistic Temperament*. New York: Free Press, 1993.

Kalat, James W. *Biological Psychology* (4th ed.). Pacific Grove, Calif.: Brooks/Cole, 1992.

Kaplan, Harold I., and Benjamin J. Sadock. *Synopsis of Psychiatry* (6th ed.). Baltimore: Williams and Wilkins, 1991.

Kazuko, Kuniyoshi. *An Overview of the Contemporary Japanese Dance Scene*. Tokyo: The Japan Foundation, 1985.

Kerr, Philip (ed.). *The Penguin Book of Lies*. New York: Viking, 1990.

Kimble, Daniel P. *Biological Psychology* (2d ed.). New York: Harcourt Brace Jovanovich College Publishers, 1992.

Kraus, Richard, Sarah Chapman Hilsendager, and Brenda Dixon. *History of the Dance in Art and Education* (3d ed.). Englewood Cliffs, N.J.: Prentice Hall, 1991.

Lazarus, Richard S. *Emotion and Adaptation*. New York: Oxford University Press, 1991.

LeDoux, Joseph E.:
"Emotion and the Amygdala." In *The Amygdala: Neurobiological Aspects of Emotion, Memory, and Mental Dysfunction*, edited by John P. Aggleton. New York: Wiley-Liss, 1992.
"Information Flow from Sensation to Emotion: Plasticity in the Neural Computation of Stimulus Value." In *Learning and Computational Neuroscience*, edited by M. Gabriel and J. Moore. Cambridge, Mass.: Bradford Books/MIT Press, 1990.

"The Neurobiology of Emotion." In *Mind and Brain: Dialogues in Cognitive Neuroscience*, edited by Joseph E. LeDoux and William Hirst. New York: Cambridge University Press, 1986.

Levinthal, Charles F. *Introduction to Physiological Psychology*. Englewood Cliffs, N.J.: Prentice Hall, 1990.

Levy, Robert I.:
"Emotion, Knowing, and Culture." In *Culture Theory: Essays on Mind, Self, and Emotion*, edited by Richard A. Shweder and Robert A. LeVine. New York: Cambridge University Press, 1984.
Tahitians: Mind and Experience in the Society Islands. Chicago: University of Chicago Press, 1973.

Lewis, Michael, and Jeannette M. Haviland (eds.). *Handbook of Emotions*. New York: Guilford Press, 1993.

Lewis, Michael, and Linda Michalson. *Children's Emotions and Moods*. New York: Plenum Press, 1983.

Liberman, Jacob. *Light-Medicine of the Future: How We Can Use It to Heal Ourselves Now*. Santa Fe, N.M.: Bear and Co., 1991.

Liebowitz, Michael R. *The Chemistry of Love*. Boston: Little, Brown, 1983.

Lingerman, Hal A. *The Healing Energies of Music*. Wheaton, Ill.: The Theosophical Publishing House, 1983.

Lutz, Catherine:
"The Domain of Emotion Words on Ifaluk." In *The Social Construction of Emotions*, edited by Rom Harré. New York: Basil Blackwell, 1986.
Unnatural Emotions. Chicago: University of Chicago Press, 1988.

Lynch, James J. *The Language of the Heart*. New York: Basic Books, 1985.

McNaughton, Neil. *Biology and Emotion*. New York: Cambridge University Press, 1989.

Marieb, Elaine N. *Human Anatomy and Physiology* (2d ed.). Redwood City, Calif.: Benjamin/Cummings, 1985.

Masters, John C., and Charles R. Carlson. "Children's and Adults' Understanding of the Causes and Consequences of Emotional States." In *Emotions, Cognition, and Behavior*, edited by Carroll E. Izard, Jerome Kagan, and Robert B. Zajonc. New York: Cambridge University Press, 1988.

Meichenbaum, Donald. *Cognitive-Behavior Modification*. New York: Plenum Press, 1977.

Menon, Usha, and Richard A. Shweder. "Kali's Tongue: Cultural Psychology and the Power of 'Shame' in Orissa, India." In *Emotions and Culture: Empirical Studies of Mutual Influence*, edited by Shinobu Kitayama and Hazel Markus. Washington, D.C.: American Psychological Association, 1994.

Morris, Desmond. *Animalwatching*. New York: Crown, 1990.

Ortony, Andrew, Gerald L. Clore, and Allan Collins. *The Cognitive Structure of Emotions*. New York: Cambridge University Press, 1988.

Patai, Raphael. *The Arab Mind*. New York: Charles Scribner's Sons, 1976.

Pickvance, Ronald. *Van Gogh in Saint-Rémy and Auvers*. New York: Metropolitan Museum of Art and Harry N. Abrams, 1986.

Plutchik, Robert:
Emotion: A Psychoevolutionary Synthesis. New York: Harper and Row, 1980.
The Emotions (rev. ed.). New York: University Press of America, 1991.
The Psychology and Biology of Emotion. New York: HarperCollins College Publishers, 1994.

Podolsky, Edward (ed.). *Music Therapy*. New York: Philosophical Library, 1954.

Restak, Richard M. *The Infant Mind*. New York: Doubleday, 1986.

Reynolds, David K. *Flowing Bridges, Quiet Waters*. Albany, N.Y.: State University of New York Press, 1989.

Robinson, David. *Living Wild*. Washington, D.C.: National Wildlife Federation, 1980.

Saarni, Carolyn, and Paul L. Harris. *Children's Understanding of Emotion*. New York: Cambridge University Press, 1989.

Scherer, Klaus R. (ed.). *Facets of Emotion*. Hillsdale, N.J.: Lawrence Erlbaum Associates, 1988.

Shaver, Phillip R., Shelley Wu, and Judith C. Schwartz. "Cross-Cultural Similarities and Differences in Emotion and Its Representation: A Prototype Approach." In *Emotion*, edited by Margaret S. Clark. Newbury Park, Calif.: Sage, 1992.

Shweder, Richard A. *Thinking Through Cultures: Expeditions in Cultural Psychology*. Cambridge, Mass.: Harvard University Press, 1991.

Simonov, Pavel Vasilevich. *The Emotional Brain*. New York: Plenum Press, 1986.

Sloboda, John A. *The Musical Mind*. Oxford, England: Clarendon Press, 1985.

Solomon, Robert C. "Getting Angry: The Jamesian Theory of Emotion in Anthropology." In *Culture Theory: Essays on Mind, Self, and Emotion*, edited by Richard A. Shweder and Robert A. LeVine. New York: Cambridge University Press, 1984.

Stearns, Carol Zisowitz, and Peter N. Stearns. *Anger: The Struggle for Emotional Control in America's History*. Chicago: University of Chicago Press, 1986.

Storr, Anthony. *Music and the Mind*. New York: Free Press, 1992.

Strayer, Janet. "Current Research in Affective Development." In *The Feeling Child: Affective Development Reconsidered*, edited by Nancy E. Curry. New York: Haworth Press, 1986.

Stuss, Donald T., and D. Frank Benson. "Emotional Concomitants of Psychosurgery." In *Neuropsychology of Human Emotion*, edited by Kenneth M. Heilman and Paul Satz. New York: Guilford Press, 1983.

Szasz, Suzanne. *The Body Language of Children*. New York: W. W. Norton, 1978.

Tavris, Carol. *Anger: The Misunderstood Emotion* (rev. ed.). New York: Touchstone, 1989.

Thompson, Jack George. *The Psychobiology of Emotions*. New York: Plenum Press, 1988.

Tortora, Gerard J., and Sandra Reynolds Grabowski. *Principles of Anatomy and Physiology* (7th ed.). New York: HarperCollins College Publishers, 1993.

Unkefer, Robert F. (ed.). *Music Therapy in the Treatment of Adults with Mental Disorders*. New York: Schirmer Books, 1990.

Vander, Arthur J., James H. Sherman, and Dorothy S. Luciano. *Human Physiology: The Mechanisms of Body Function* (5th ed.). New York: McGraw-Hill, 1990.

Willemsen, Eleanor. *Understanding Infancy*. San Francisco: W. H. Freeman, 1979.

Wolff, Peter H. *The Development of Behavioral States and the Expression of Emotions in Early Infancy*. Chicago: University of Chicago Press, 1987.

Woodham-Smith, Cecil. *Queen Victoria: From Her Birth to the Death of the Prince Consort*. New York: Alfred A. Knopf, 1972.

PERIODICALS

Abu-Lughod, Lila. "Honor and the Sentiments of Loss in a Bedouin Society." *American Ethnologist*, May 1985.

Asher, Jules. "Born to Be Shy?" *Psychology Today*, Apr. 1987.

"Back in Uniform." *Time*, June 30, 1961.

Barasch, Marc. "Welcome to the Mind-Body Revolution." *Psychology Today*, July/Aug. 1993.

Berenson, F. M. "Emotions and Rationality." *International Journal of Moral and Social Studies*, Spring 1991.

Church, George J. "An End to the Long Ordeal." *Time*, Feb. 2, 1981.

Davidson, Richard J., et al. "Approach-Withdrawal and Cerebral Asymmetry: Emotional Expression and Brain Physiology I." *Journal of Personality and Social Psychology*, 1990, Vol. 58, no. 2, pp. 330-341.

Derryberry, Douglas, and Don M. Tucker. "Neural Mechanisms of Emotion." *Journal of Consulting and Clinical Psychology*, 1992, Vol. 60, no. 3, pp. 329-338.

Diamond, Jared. "Sex and the Female Agenda." *Discover*, Sept. 1993.

Doerner, William R. "A Scandal That Will Not Die." *Time*, Apr. 24, 1989.

Ekman, Paul:

"Are There Basic Emotions?" *Psychological Review*, 1992, Vol. 99, no. 3, pp. 550-553.

"An Argument for Basic Emotions." *Cognition and Emotion*, 1992, Vol. 6, no. 3/4, pp. 169-200.

"Facial Expressions of Emotion: New Findings, New Questions." *Psychological Review*, Jan. 1992.

Farwell, Lawrence A., and Emanuel Donchin. "The Truth Will Out: Interrogative Polygraphy ('Lie Detection') with Event-Related Brain Potentials." *Psychophysiology*, Sept. 1991.

Ganchrow, Judith R., Jacob E. Steiner, and Munif Daher. "Neonatal Facial Expressions in Response to Different Qualities and Intensities of Gustatory Stimuli." *Infant Behavior and Development*, 1983, Vol. 6, pp. 473-484.

Gest, Ted. "The Bizarre and Troubling Escapades of Mayor Barry." *U.S. News and World Report*, Jan. 9, 1989.

Goode, Erica E., with Joannie M. Schrof and Sarah Burke. "Where Emotions Come From." *U.S. News and World Report*, June 24, 1991.

Hayes, Donald S., and Dina M. Casey. "Young Children and Television: The Retention of Emotional Reactions." *Child Development*, Dec. 1992.

Hopson, Janet L. "A Pleasurable Chemistry." *Psychology Today*, July/Aug. 1988.

Izard, Carroll E.:

"Facial Expressions and the Regulation of Emotions." *Journal of Personality and Social Psychology*, 1990, Vol. 58, no. 3, pp. 487-498.

"Four Systems for Emotion Activation: Cognitive and Noncognitive Processes." *Psychological Review*, 1993, Vol. 100, no. 1, pp. 68-90.

Kahn, Herman. "The Japanese Character." *Psychology Today*, Mar. 1973.

Kalin, Ned H. "The Neurobiology of Fear." *Scientific American*, May 1993.

Kolbert, Elizabeth. "When Baring All to Four Million Viewers Doesn't Help." *New York Times*, July 18, 1993.

Kora, Takehisa, and Kenshiro Ohara. "Morita Therapy." *Psychology Today*, Mar. 1973.

Kristof, Nicholas D. "Chinese Find Their Voice: A Radio Call-In Show." *New York Times*, Apr. 26, 1993.

Lawrence, Susan V. "Dr. Ruth, Beijing Style." *U.S. News and World Report*, May 17, 1993.

Leary, Mark R., et al. "Social Blushing." *Psychological Bulletin*, 1992, Vol. 112, no. 3, pp. 446-460.

LeDoux, Joseph E.:

"Brain Mechanisms of Emotion and Emotional Learning." *Current Opinion in Neurobiology*, 1992, Vol. 2, pp. 191-197.

"Cognitive-Emotional Interactions in the Brain." *Cognition and Emotion*, 1989, Vol. 3, pp. 267-289.

Leviton, Richard. "Healing Vibrations." *Yoga Journal*, Jan./Feb. 1994.

Levy, Bernard I. "Research into the Psychological Meaning of Color." *American Journal of Art Therapy*, Jan. 1984.

Lutz, Catherine, and Geoffrey M. White. "The Anthropology of Emotions." *Annual Review of Anthropology*, 1986, Vol. 15, pp. 405-436.

MacLeod, Scott. "Sand in a Well-Oiled Machine." *Time*, May 8, 1989.

Markus, Hazel Rose, and Shinobu Kitayama. "Culture and the Self: Implications for Cognition, Emotion, and Motivation." *Psychological Review*, 1991, Vol. 98, no. 2, pp. 224-253.

Martin, Bradley, Bill Powell, and Hideko Takayama. "Takeshita Bows Out." *Newsweek*, May 8, 1989.

Mazur, Allen, and Theodore A. Lamb. "Testosterone, Status, and Mood in Human Males." *Hormones and Behavior*, 1980, Vol. 14, pp. 236-246.

Meredith, Nikki. "Stage Fright's Tyranny of Terror." *Washington Post*, Oct. 2, 1986.

Mesquita, Batja, and Nico H. Frijda. "Cultural Variations in Emotions: A Review." *Psychological Bulletin*, 1992, Vol. 112, no. 2, pp. 179-204.

Mestel, Rosie. "We're All Connected." *Discover*, Jan. 1994.

Miller, Laurence. "The Emotional Brain." *Psychology Today*, Feb. 1988.

"Mixed Verdict, Divided City." *Time*, Aug. 20, 1990.

Motley, Michael T. "Taking the Terror Out of Talk." *Psychology Today*, Jan. 1988.

Newman, Judith. "Are They Crazy? Why Do People Tell All on Talk Shows?" *Cosmopolitan*, Aug. 1992.

Novaco, Raymond W. "Treatment of Chronic Anger through Cognitive and Relaxation Controls." *Journal of Consulting and Clinical Psychology*, 1976, Vol. 44, no. 4, p. 681.

Ogilvie, Bruce C. "Stimulus Addiction: The Sweet Psychic Jolt of Danger." *Psychology Today*, Oct. 1974.

Plutchik, Robert. "A Language for the Emotions." *Psychology Today*, Feb. 1980.

"The Primal Screamer." *Newsweek*, Apr. 12, 1971.

Roberts, Marjory. "No Language but a Cry." *Psychology Today*, June 1987.

Rose, Robert M., Irwin S. Bernstein, and Thomas P. Gordon. "Consequences of Social Conflict on Plasma Testosterone Levels in Rhesus Monkeys." *Psychosomatic Medicine*, Jan./Feb. 1975.

Russell, James A.:

"Culture and the Categorization of Emotions." *Psychological Bulletin*, 1991, Vol. 110, no. 3, pp. 426-450.

"The Preschooler's Understanding of the Causes and Consequences of Emotion." *Child Development*, Dec. 1992.

Schimmel, Solomon. "Anger and Its Control in Graeco-Roman and Modern Psychology." *Psychiatry*, Nov. 1979.

Schwartz, John. "Putting a Certain Face on Emotions." *Washington Post*, Nov. 8, 1993.

"Seven Tumultuous Days." *Time*, Nov. 5, 1973.

Solomon, Robert C. "Emotions and Anthropology: The Logic of Emotional World Views." *Inquiry*, 1978, Vol. 21, pp. 181-199.

Stearns, Peter N., and Carol Zisowitz Stearns. "Emotionology: Clarifying the History of Emotions and Emotional Standards." *American Historical Review*, Oct. 1985.

Stearns, Peter N., and Deborah C. Stearns. "Biology and Culture: Toward a New Combination." *Contention*, Dec. 1993.

Tomarken, Andrew J., et al. "Individual Differences in Anterior Brain Asymmetry and Fundamental Dimensions of Emo-

tion." *Journal of Personality and Social Psychology*, April 1992.

Waldholz, Michael. "Panic Pathway: Study of Fear Shows Emotions Can Alter 'Wiring' of the Brain." *Wall Street Journal*, Sept. 29, 1993.

Witkin, Gordon. "The Hunt for a Better Lie Detector." U.S. *News and World Report*, June 14, 1993.

Zillmann, Dolf, and Jennings Bryant. "Effect of Residual Excitation on the Emotional Response to Provocation and Delayed Aggressive Behavior." *Journal of Personality and Social Psychology*, 1974, Vol. 30, no. 6,

pp. 782-791.

Zillmann, Dolf, Rolland C. Johnson, and Kenneth D. Day. "Attribution of Apparent Arousal and Proficiency of Recovery from Sympathetic Activation Affecting Excitation Transfer to Aggressive Behavior." *Journal of Experimental Social Psychology*, 1974, Vol. 10, pp. 503-515.

OTHER SOURCES

"Interviewing and Interrogation: The Reid Technique." Facilitator Guide. Minneapolis: Law Enforcement Resource Center and John E. Reid and Associates, 1991.

INDEX

ACKNOWLEDGMENTS

The Editors of E*motions* wish to thank these individuals for their valuable contributions:

Penguin Books, USA, for quotes from T*he Iliad* by Homer (appearing on pages 105, 106, and 126), translated by Robert Fagles, translation copyright © 1990 by Robert Fagles. Introduction and Notes copyright © by Bernard Knox. Used by permission of Viking Penguin, a division of Penguin Books USA Inc.

Lila Abu-Lughod, New York University, New York; Kim Bard, Emory University, Atlanta; Laura Betzig, University of Michigan, Ann Arbor; Joseph P. Buckley III, John E. Reid and Associates, Inc., Chicago; Gordon Burghardt, University of Tennessee, Knoxville; Brooks Burr, Southern Illinois University, Carbondale; Manfred Clynes, Sonoma, Calif.; Philippe Dacla, CNRI, Paris; Michael Davis, Yale University, New Haven, Conn.; Janis Driscoll, University of Colorado, Denver; Helen Fisher, American Museum of Natural History, New York; William Frey, Ramsey Medical Center, St. Paul; Bill Fry, Stanford University, Palo Alto, Calif.; Gordon Gallup, State University of New York, Albany; Neil Greenberg, University of Tennessee, Knoxville; Harry Jaffe, Washington, D.C.; Kay Jamison, Johns Hopkins University, Baltimore; Ned H. Kalin, University of Wisconsin, Madison; Robert Levy, Chapel Hill, N.C.; Catherine Lutz, University of North Carolina, Chapel Hill; Usha Menon, University of Chicago; Paul K. Minor, American International Security Corporation, Fairfax, Va.; John Moffett, Georgetown University, Washington, D.C.; Peter Moller, American Museum of Natural History, New York; David K. Reynolds, Center for Constructive Living, Coos Bay, Oreg.; James Russell, University of British Columbia, Vancouver; Lauren V. Scharf, Seattle; Phillip R. Shaver, University of California, Davis; Richard Shweder, University of Chicago; Sharon Smith, Federal Bureau of Investigation, Washington, D.C.; Carol Z. Stearns, Pittsburgh; Peter N. Stearns, Carnegie-Mellon University, Pittsburgh; Jack Thompson, Centre College, Danville, Ky.; Ethel Tobach, American Museum of Natural History, New York; Sean Williams, Evergreen State College, Olympia, Wash.

PICTURE CREDITS

Cover: Bob Martin/Allsport, London. **7:** Stan Grossfeld/Boston Globe—John Dominis/Life Magazine, © Time Warner—Peter Charlesworth/JB Pictures—Malcolm Linton/Black Star. **8, 9:** Henry Grossman. **10:** Mike Wells/Aspect Picture Library, London. **14, 15:** Art by Stephen R. Wagner. **16:** Stan Grossfeld/Boston Globe. **17:** © Gale Zucker. **19:** Scott Camazine/Science Source/Photo Researchers. **21:** Michael Klausman/NYT Pictures. **22, 23:** Michael Ochs Archives, Venice, Calif. **26:** Jonnie Miles/Photonica. **28, 29:** Background Torregano/Sipa-Press. John Eastcott/Woodfin Camp & Associates—M. P. Kahl/Okapia—A. Huber/Okapia. **30, 31:** © Frank Siteman/Light Sources Stock; Brian Vikander/Westlight. **32, 33:** Evan H. Sheppard; Mark S. Wexler/Woodfin Camp & Associates. **34, 35:** Evan H. Sheppard; Lila Abu-Lughod/Anthro-Photo. **36, 37:** Evan H. Sheppard; Laura Betzig. **38, 39:** Evan H. Sheppard; Richard A. Shweder and Usha Menon; Richard A. Shweder. **40, 41:** John Dominis, Life Magazine, © Time Warner. **42, 43:** By permission of the Syndics of Cambridge University Library, Cambridge, England, except bottom right, *The Expressions of the Emotions in Man and Animals* by Charles Darwin (John Murray, 1892). **44:** Imperial War Museum, London; Bundesarchiv, Koblenz. **47:** Dr. Kim Bard, Yerkes Regional Primate Research Center of Emory University, Atlanta. **48:** George McCarthy, Bruce Coleman Limited, Uxbridge, Middlesex—Keith Scholey/Planet Earth Pictures, London; David Horwell/Planet Earth Pictures, London. **49:** Michael Fogden/Oxford Scientific Films, Long Hanborough, Oxfordshire—Jean-Paul Ferrero/Ardea Photographics, London. **50, 51:** Ned H. Kalin, M.D., Department of Psychiatry, University of Wisconsin-Madison Medical School. **55:** Wolfgang Weinhäupl/Okapia. **57:** Fox Movietone News—Ken Regan/Camera 5. **59:** Daniel Simon/Gamma-Liaison International. **60, 61:** Paul Ekman, Ph.D., School of Medicine, Psychiatry Department, University of California, San Francisco. **63:** Suzanne Szasz. **64:** Anita K. Stein—inset David Grossman/Photo Researchers. **65:** Taste-induced facial expressions in neonates, prior to first feeding experience. J. E. Steiner, *Infant Behavior and Development*, Vol.6, 1983; Anita K. Stein. **66:** Pongsak Dej-Udom—insets Michael Newman/Photoedit; Stanley Goldberg; Fatima Taylor. **67:** Courtesy Lynn Borton and David Kolker; Charles Thatcher/Tony Stone; Catherine Bly Cox. **68, 69:** Suzanne Szasz (2)—Ursula Markus/Photo Researchers; Fatima Taylor. **70, 71:** Susie Fitzhugh; inset Darcie Conner Johnston; David Young-Wolff/Photoedit—Suzanne Szasz. **72, 73:** Photos by Fil Hunter, photo montage by Barbara M. Sheppard. **75:** Allsport, London. **76, 77:** AP/Wide World Photos. **78, 79:** Peter Charlesworth/JB Pictures. **81:** Francois Rickard/Allsport. **84:** Charts by Time-Life Books, courtesy Dr. Manfred Clynes. **86:** © Jack Vartoogian. **87:** © Jack Vartoogian; Theo Westenberger/Gamma-Liaison International. **91:** Archives of the History of American Psychology, Akron, Ohio. **95-103:** Art by Alfred T. Kamajian. **104, 105:** Malcolm Linton/Black Star. **110:** Gerald French/FPG International. **112:** Nicolas Luttiau/Pressesports, Cedex, France. **117:** From *Synopsis of Psychiatry: Behavioral Sciences, Clinical Psychiatry* by Harold I. Kaplan, M.D., and Benjamin J. Sadock, M.D., Williams & Wilkins, Baltimore, 1991. **118:** L.R. Baxter, M.D., UCLA School of Medicine. **119:** Painting by Vincent van Gogh, the Phillips Collection, Washington D.C.—painting by Vincent van Gogh, © Rijksdienst Beeldende Kunst's Gravenhage Inv. nk 2511. **120:** Brett Telegan/© 1994 The Walt Disney Co., reprinted with permission of Discover Magazine. **122:** Masaaki Kazama/Photonica. **127:** Sally and Richard Greenhill, London. **128, 129:** Photos from *The Player*, courtesy of After Dark Productions and Fine Line Features. © 1992 After Dark Productions, Inc. All rights reserved. **130, 131:** Polygraph by Paul Minor—Lawrence A. Farwell, Ph.D. (3). **132, 133:** David Hume Kennerly/Time Magazine (4)—Mitsuhiro Wada/Gamma-Liaison International; AP/Wide World Photos; Evan H. Sheppard.